D0354306

ADVANCE PRAISE

"If you want to improve your business, this is the book to read. The ideas developed by the authors have worked everywhere I've seen them applied."
— James M. Kilts, former Chairman and CEO of Gillette, CEO and President of Nabisco, and President of Kraft USA

"In *Beliefs, Behaviors and Results*, the authors show how they have helped my organization and many others establish the strategies and capabilities that are critical to driving and sustaining superior performance."
— Don Knauss, Chairman and CEO of the Clorox Company

"Many organizations operate with inconsistent and confused beliefs that produce ineffective behaviors and suboptimal outcomes. This book helps define the process for significantly improving results by strategically focusing on productive beliefs and behavior. These concepts contributed to our success at BB&T."
— John Allison, former Chairman and CEO of BB&T and Chairman of the CATO Institute

"Gillis, Mergy, and Shalleck have a very clear vision of what's most important in leading and managing a business and how that's achieved. Their analysis is insightful and their conclusions instructive and practical. This is a high-value read for any current or future business leader who wants to do it right—to take good care of all the enterprise's constituencies and achieve the ultimate goal: delivering sustainable economic profit growth."
— Miles D. White, Chairman and CEO of Abbott Laboratories

"A terrific blueprint for setting the tone at the top in pursuit of superior performance in both the customer markets and the capital markets in a synergistic and enduring fashion."

> —Douglas R. Conant, former President, CEO, and director of the Campbell Soup Company and *New York Times* bestselling coauthor of *TouchPoints*

"Real progress is made through tackling the important issues successfully. Leaders who have embraced the concepts and principles in *Beliefs, Behaviors, and Results* have repeatedly shown how lasting this transformation can be."

> —Travis Engen, former CEO of Alcan and ITT Industries

"The valuable guidance in *Beliefs, Behaviors, and Results* makes the book a must-read for leaders seeking to maximize shareholder returns. At MWV, we have successfully implemented the authors' system with exceptional results."

> —John Luke, Chairman and CEO of MWV

BELIEFS,
BEHAVIORS,
&
RESULTS

BELIEFS, BEHAVIORS, & RESULTS

THE CHIEF EXECUTIVE'S GUIDE TO DELIVERING SUPERIOR SHAREHOLDER VALUE

SCOTT GILLIS, LEE MERGY, JOE SHALLECK

GREENLEAF
BOOK GROUP PRESS

This publication is designed to provide accurate and authoritative information in regard to the subject matter covered. It is sold with the understanding that the publisher and author are not engaged in rendering legal or accounting services. If legal advice or other expert assistance is required, the services of a competent professional should be sought.

Published by Greenleaf Book Group Press
Austin, Texas
www.gbgpress.com

Copyright ©2013 MS Galt & Company, LLC

All rights reserved.

No part of this book may be reproduced, stored in a retrieval system, or transmitted by any means, electronic, mechanical, photocopying, recording, or otherwise, without written permission from the copyright holder.

Distributed by Greenleaf Book Group LLC

For ordering information or special discounts for bulk purchases, please contact Greenleaf Book Group LLC at PO Box 91869, Austin, TX 78709, 512.891.6100.

Design and composition by Greenleaf Book Group LLC
Cover design by Greenleaf Book Group LLC

Publisher's Cataloging-In-Publication Data
(Prepared by The Donohue Group, Inc.)

Gillis, Scott, 1956-
    Beliefs, behaviors, & results : the chief executive's guide to delivering superior shareholder value / Scott Gillis, Lee Mergy, Joe Shalleck.—1st ed.
        p. : ill., charts ; cm.
    Issued also as an ebook.
    ISBN: 978-1-60832-428-6
    1. Leadership. 2. Corporate culture. 3. Organizational effectiveness. 4. Chief executive officers. 5. Success in business. 6. Stockholder wealth. I. Mergy, Lee. II. Shalleck, Joe. III. Title. IV. Title: Beliefs, behaviors, and results

HD57.7 .G555 2013
658.4/092   2012945615

Part of the Tree Neutral® program, which offsets the number of trees consumed in the production and printing of this book by taking proactive steps, such as planting trees in direct proportion to the number of trees used: www.treeneutral.com

Printed in the United States of America on acid-free paper   TreeNeutral®

12 13 14 15 16 17   10 9 8 7 6 5 4 3 2 1

First Edition

With sincere appreciation to all the chief executives whom we have had the privilege of serving and from whom we have learned so much.

Contents

Acknowledgments

We want to extend our thanks to Larry Jones, Michael Choo, John Reuter, and our other colleagues at Galt & Company, whose innumerable contributions made this book possible.

INTRODUCTION
What You Will Learn from This Book

From religion to politics, all human endeavors are strongly influenced by beliefs. *Beliefs* drive *behaviors*, which in turn drive *results*. It therefore should come as no surprise that differences in management beliefs play a large role in explaining differences in business performance.

> **Beliefs ➡ Behaviors ➡ Results**

This book focuses on the beliefs and behaviors of some of the most admired and best performing Fortune 200 companies and their chief executives. It explains how these leaders have established a culture and approach to management that has enabled their companies to both

- *"Win" in the customer markets* by doing a better job of creating customer value.
- *"Win" in the capital markets* by doing a better job of capturing customer value for the company's shareholders.

Throughout this book, you will hear directly from some of the world's most successful CEOs. These CEOs will explain the core philosophy behind their success and provide examples of how that philosophy has influenced their decisions and the decisions and actions of their entire organizations.

Who are these chief executives? They are leaders like:

- The late Roberto Goizueta, who reinvented Coca-Cola, delivering annual total shareholder returns of 27 percent annually over his seventeen-year tenure.

- Jim Kilts, who as CEO turned around the performance of three of the world's most notable consumer brand companies: Kraft Foods, Nabisco, and Gillette.

- Travis Engen, who transformed ITT Industries, increasing its shareholder value threefold before leaving to become chief executive of Alcan, where he doubled shareholder value within four years.

- The late Sir Brian Pitman, who doubled the market capitalization of Lloyds Bank every three years over a fifteen-year time span.

- John Allison and Kelly King, who, as a team, grew BB&T from a small North Carolina regional bank with $4.5 billion in assets to the tenth largest financial services holding company headquartered in the United States.

- Don Knauss, who reenergized Minute Maid, reversed the erosion of Coca-Cola's share of profits in North America, and went on to revitalize the shareholder performance of the Clorox Company.

- Miles White, who as CEO of Abbott Laboratories for the past thirteen years has outperformed his peers in the health care and pharmaceutical industries.

- John Luke, who transformed MeadWestvaco from a mid-sized forest and paper products company into a profitable global packaging company generating leading shareholder returns.

These chief executives have a tremendous track record of creating value for their customers and wealth for their shareholders. Had you invested in this group of companies when these CEOs began implementing the principles contained in this book, you would have earned, on average, 90 percent more on your investment over the next five years than if you had invested in an index of their industry peers. (See Figure 0.1[1].)

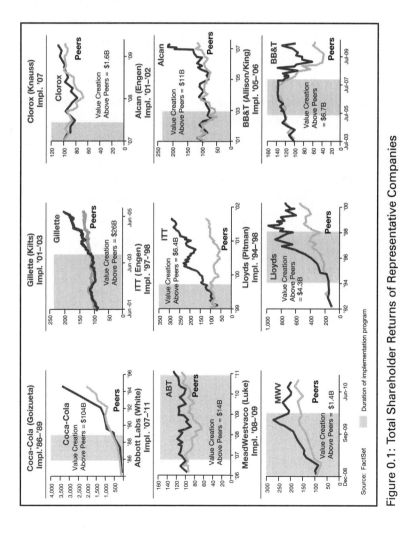

Figure 0.1: Total Shareholder Returns of Representative Companies

Shareholder performance is the ultimate measure of corporate success. There are many other metrics and constituents that need to be considered in managing a corporation; however, shareholders are the subordinate beneficiaries of corporate success. No company can sustain superior shareholder returns if it is not delivering exceptional value to its customers, and no company can continue to deliver exceptional returns to its shareholders unless it is able to attract and retain talented employees. In fact, the CEOs profiled in this book not only consider shareholder returns as an ultimate measure of their success, but they also consider the pursuit of superior shareholder returns to be the governing objective of their companies. As you will read, companies that are able to deliver consistently superior shareholder value growth end up developing a reinvestment advantage that is difficult for competitors to match.

Almost every chief executive is focused on delivering superior returns for their shareholders. Yet, few corporations have actually done so, let alone sustained that performance for any length of time. In fact over the last thirty years, only 2 percent of Fortune 500 companies have been able to deliver shareholder returns in the top quartile of their industry for five consecutive years. Why? Well, most academics will cite the overwhelming force of competition that constantly works to level the playing field and revert the performance of any company to the mean. However, while competitive forces exist, this response ignores the performance of chief executives who have delivered returns far in excess of their peers over extended periods of time and, in some cases, for more than one company during their careers.

These CEOs will tell you that it is not competition that places the greatest limits on corporate performance, rather it is management misconceptions about what actually drives shareholder value and how to effectively manage its growth that is the most significant deterrent.

> "Internal management misconceptions, not external competition, are the most significant impediments to improving shareholder value."
> —Jim Kilts, former Chairman and Chief Executive of Gillette, President and Chief Executive of Nabisco, and President of Kraft USA

Managers in every corporation carry with them deeply held beliefs about how their company should be run. Some of these beliefs are rules of thumb accumulated over years of industry experience, while others have been absorbed from their mentors. Yet, few of these beliefs are the outcome of deliberate efforts to create as much wealth as possible for shareholders. As a result, many of these beliefs are standing in the way of doing so.

Throughout this book, the featured CEOs will emphasize that sustainable improvements in corporate performance begin by confronting management misconceptions and establishing the right set of beliefs. After all, it is these beliefs that influence the behaviors of hundreds, if not thousands, of managers across an organization and ultimately determine the results a corporation delivers over time.

The most successful CEOs not only think and act like owners, but they also cause managers across their companies to do the same. Not by demanding their employees slavishly execute their directives, but by establishing a set of guiding principles and organizational conditions that support superior decision making and execution.

Achieving that degree of intellectual and philosophical alignment in large organizations is not easy. However, the chief executives featured in this book will describe and demonstrate how to do just that. While the styles of these successful CEOs are as different as their personalities, they share a common set of beliefs and management principles that are at the heart of their success. This means that what has worked for them will work for you.

HOW THIS BOOK CAN HELP YOU

Several books have been written on the subject of corporate performance and managing shareholder value. Most of them are academic in nature, focused on financial theory, analytical frameworks and strategic rules of thumb that are best taught in business schools. This book is different. It is written from the perspective of some of the world's most successful CEOs.

Why this focus on CEOs? It's simple. Only chief executives can impact the beliefs and behaviors of an entire corporation. Only they can establish the governance conditions and standards that affect the decisions and actions of hundreds of other managers across an entire company. And only they can produce the degree of corporate-wide change required to achieve and sustain superior shareholder returns over time.

We have spent our professional lives working with and studying some of the best shareholder-value-managed companies in the world and have witnessed, firsthand, both the actions that have worked for the best leaders and the pitfalls experienced by their less successful peers. We have continued to chisel away to find the essence of what drives corporate success and have discovered that superior performance is the result of a disciplined approach to management, and the resulting culture that this discipline creates.

One CEO commented that the idea of examining and then discarding everything that didn't work was reminiscent of the approach Michelangelo purportedly took in creating his statue of *David*.

"How," wondered Pope Julius II, who commissioned the work, "did you create such a masterpiece as *David*, Michelangelo?" The artist replied, "I simply chipped away everything that was not David."

We are no Michelangelos, but we have had the privilege of working with some of the true masters of leadership and shareholder value creation. We have studied what has worked for them and we have been able to help other leaders institutionalize these principles in their own companies.

What This Book Is and Is Not All About

This is a book about

- Overcoming the internal impediments to superior performance
- Aligning everyone in your organization around a common objective and approach to managing the business
- Creating an enduring "ownership" culture
- Delivering and sustaining superior profit growth and shareholder value

This is not a book about

- Measurement and valuation methodologies
- Analytical models and equations
- Stock market forecasts or strategic postulates

CONTENT AND STRUCTURE

This book is structured around the five core beliefs these successful executives have used to shape and guide their organizations.

Chapter 1 provides an overview of these five principles and the common misconceptions that prevent most management teams from achieving superior shareholder returns.

Chapters 2 through 6 are written from the perspectives of chief executives who have transformed the culture of their companies and delivered superior shareholder returns as a result. Through their words and case examples, you will gain a clear picture of how the five principles are applied in practice. In each chapter you will read about

- *What's required:* the most important concepts these successful CEOs have used to improve the value of their companies.

- *Where companies go wrong:* common misconceptions and mistakes other companies make that detract from shareholder value.

- *Key takeaways:* steps you should consider to improve the value of your company.

Chapter 7 describes the most important success factors and the common pitfalls chief executives encounter in transforming their corporations and lays out the common elements of the change-management blueprints employed by successful corporations.

CHAPTER 1
Explaining Our Central Theme: How Beliefs Impact Behaviors and Results

. . . .

"Leadership is about instilling the *beliefs* and *behaviors* that produce desired *results*."

—John Allison, former Chairman and Chief Executive, BB&T

. . . .

- Although external competitive forces are constantly working against a company's growth in shareholder value, it is the internal misconceptions that exist within management that place the greatest limitations on corporate performance.

- Improving shareholder value is about overcoming these misconceptions and establishing the beliefs and behaviors that lead to superior results in both the customer and capital markets.

- Ensuring that employees truly know what leads to superior performance and how to put those principles into practice is one of the most important roles of the chief executive and their management teams.

WHAT IS SUPERIOR PERFORMANCE?

If asked, the senior management teams of virtually every publicly traded company will say that they are focused on delivering superior shareholder returns. Yet very few companies have been able to outperform their peers consistently over extended periods of time.

Over the past twenty years, the average company in the S&P 500 delivered total shareholder returns (TSRs, or stock price appreciation plus dividend yield) of about 10 percent annually. In other words, $100 invested in the average S&P 500 company today would be worth $110 a year later. At that rate of return, it would take approximately 7 to 8 years for a company to double its shareholder value.

If we group companies within an industry into quartiles, however, as we do in Figure 1.1, those firms in the top 25 percent did significantly better, with most generating TSRs of 16 percent to 20 percent. In effect, companies in the top quartile have doubled their shareholder value in 4 to 5 years.

Why is this gap so large? What distinguishes chief executives and companies that have been able to consistently deliver shareholder returns in the top quartile of their peer group from those that have not? Is it product innovation? The assets the company controls? The market share position it has built? Or is superior performance just a statistical phenomenon that is difficult, if not impossible, to either predict or replicate?

Based on nearly twenty-five years of working with some of the world's best-run companies, we have learned that *superior performance is not random; it can be managed.* More specifically, what we have observed is that superior performance is the result of a disciplined approach to management and the resulting culture that this discipline creates. Underpinning this discipline is a set of beliefs that the CEOs, along with the senior management teams, have

1991-2011 (20 Years)	Total Shareholder Returns		
	Top Quartile	Median	Bottom Quartile
Semiconductors & Equipment	20.4%	13.8%	3.1%
Energy	18.2%	13.6%	5.0%
Diversified Financials	19.4%	13.5%	6.0%
Real Estate	16.1%	12.4%	5.9%
Transportation	19.9%	11.7%	6.4%
Healthcare Equipment & Services	19.1%	11.5%	3.7%
Household & Personal Products	13.1%	11.5%	8.8%
Software & Services	20.8%	11.4%	2.8%
Capital Goods	18.0%	11.0%	3.8%
Technology Hardware & Equipment	20.6%	10.8%	3.5%
Retailing	18.5%	10.3%	0.6%
Automobiles & Components	20.1%	9.8%	1.0%
Consumer Services	15.9%	9.8%	3.6%
Media	16.2%	9.7%	1.2%
Consumer Durables & Apparel	16.6%	9.6%	-0.1%
Utilities	13.0%	9.4%	5.6%
Pharm, Bio & Life Sciences	18.1%	9.3%	3.0%
Banks	15.4%	9.2%	3.1%
Food, Beverage & Tobacco	17.2%	9.2%	3.3%
Insurance	15.7%	9.0%	2.2%
Food & Staples Retailing	13.4%	9.0%	4.8%
Commercial & Professional Services	17.2%	8.7%	2.2%
Materials	16.0%	8.1%	2.1%
Telecommunication Services	9.8%	7.8%	-0.6%
S&P 500	17.2%	9.8%	3.2%

Source: FactSet

Figure 1.1: Range of Shareholder Returns by Industry, 1991–2011

instilled in their organizations. Those beliefs drive behaviors, which in turn drive the outstanding results these companies have been able to achieve.

Superior Performance Is Not a Random Walk

In his now classic book, *A Random Walk Down Wall Street*, Princeton economics professor Burton Malkiel argues that stock prices typically follow a "random walk" in their day-to-day fluctuations. As a result, investors cannot consistently outperform market averages.

However, over longer periods of time, chief executives of well-run companies are able to deliver superior shareholder returns relative to peers within their industry. Why? These CEOs don't get caught up in chasing all revenue growth or quarterly EPS goals. Instead, they put in place the standards and capabilities that allow their organizations to differentiate between value-creating and value-consuming investments and they focus their strategies on delivering consistently superior cash flow and shareholder value growth.

CHECK YOUR PREMISE

"I know what increases shareholder value," many managers say. "I hire good people who make good products and deliver outstanding service, which leads to satisfied customers. That in turn generates healthy earnings growth and solid increases in our stock price."

As a general rule of thumb, that is correct. But not all customers and investments are profitable. So, yes, you want to hire good people and you want those good people to make good products that satisfy customers. But you also want your people to understand fully how their decisions and actions link to and drive profitability and cash flow. You don't want your advertising manager spending all their time thinking about boosting shareholder value. But you do want to make sure that the majority of advertising investment is driving profitable growth.

The idea of hiring good people who make good products leads us in the right direction, but it is not specific enough. As we will see in a moment, there is a single path that will lead to maximum shareholder value. But as you move down it, there may be scores of different decisions that a wide range of employees will have to make. The odds are very small that they will make all those decisions correctly without a specific set of principles that they can follow.

It makes much more sense for senior management to explain to employees:

- What drives shareholder value.
- How to determine where and why shareholder value is being created and consumed.
- How to use this information to make better strategic and resource allocation decisions and deliver higher levels of profit growth and cash flow.

WHERE COMPANIES GO WRONG: COMMON MISCONCEPTIONS

Correcting management misconceptions about what drives shareholder value and how to effectively grow it is the first step toward producing superior shareholder returns. What are some of those misconceptions? Let's highlight a couple of the more chronic ones.

Believing All Growth Is Good

Markets are not homogeneous, yet most managers consider all share points to be valuable and believe that all revenue growth is good.

Few management teams appreciate just how much profit margins and cash flow vary by product category, customer segment, channel, geographic region and activity across the value chain.

While most management teams segment their markets by consumer, product, or channel to better understand customers' needs, few managers go through the effort of measuring the profitability those market segments generate today or can generate in the future.

As a result, most management teams are reduced to managing a business profitability by aggregated financial line item. When viewing the averages, all revenues look good, all costs look bad, and the opportunities to better manage the business mix are not seen, let alone acted upon.

From an aggregate line-item perspective, there is a strong bias to achieve revenue share leadership. After all, doesn't market share leadership generate significant competitive advantages such as economies of scale, being top of mind with consumers, and gaining leverage with the trade? And don't these advantages naturally lead to superior financial results?

The answer to both questions is: not necessarily. Blind pursuit of market share makes a critical and often painfully incorrect assumption that all points of market share contribute to shareholder value.

You have to overcome what Sir Brian Pitman, former Chairman and CEO of Lloyds TSB, calls with a great degree of irony, "the Institutional Imperative."

"There is a propensity to grow, regardless of the consequences to the shareholder. It is present in all companies, even the best managed. It is an extremely tenacious force that works incessantly against achieving superior shareholder returns. Not all growth is good. Your focus must be on the things that increase shareholder value," said Pitman.

It is not the case that Pitman was antigrowth. He was just much more clear than most about what his company was focused on growing: shareholder value.

You may be surprised to learn that in many Fortune 200 companies, less than 40 percent of the company's employed capital is generating over 100 percent of its shareholder value, while 25 percent to 35 percent of its employed capital is actually destroying shareholder value!

When you think about that statement, you can begin to appreciate the enormous leverage that exists to improve the shareholder value of most corporations. Companies can often double shareholder value by redirecting resources (both capital and people) to more aggressively grow those parts of the company that are contributing to shareholder value while reducing investment in those areas that are not.

Believing That EPS Growth Alone Drives Shareholder Value

Most management teams are convinced that growth in earnings per share drives their companies' stock prices. (After all, this seems to be the only thing sell-side analysts talk about.) The reasoning goes something like this: "I have a price-to-earnings multiple of 15; the market values companies like ours with P/E ratios between 14 and 16. So improving shareholder value isn't that complicated: we'll grow our earnings, multiply those earnings per share by our P/E multiple, and that will determine our stock price. The analysts rarely ask about the balance sheet if we don't carry too much debt and don't make any acquisitions that would dilute earnings."

Appealing as that logic may seem, it is wrong. Most managers are surprised to learn that not all EPS growth improves shareholder value. Actions that increase earnings can actually consume shareholder value if those actions compromise the company's future cash flow potential. How often have you seen shortsighted managers chase EPS growth by cutting back on necessary reinvestment or reducing marketing and R&D spending in order to make next quarter's earnings target? How often have you seen acquisitions that are accretive to earnings but do not generate an adequate return on the capital invested to make the acquisition? And how often have you seen managers "invest for the long term" by pouring capital into declining businesses only to see future cash flows continue to deteriorate?

Earnings Are Made Up, Cash Flow Is Real

Roberto Goizueta, one of the greatest creators of shareholder value of all time, was asked to describe how he had been so successful at growing the value of the Coca-Cola Company. He said he learned it from his grandfather, who used to say: "I am a great believer in cash flow. Earnings are a man-made convention, but cash is cash. The larger the company is, the less it understands cash flow. The smaller the business, the better it understands cash flow."

Cash flow, not earnings, drives shareholder value. And the capital requirements of a company (or business) have a direct impact on the percentage of earnings that is translated into cash flow.

A more accurate measure of profitability, from the shareholder's perspective, is called economic profit.[3] Economic profit is the earnings generated by a company (or business) minus a charge for the capital employed to generate those earnings. As we will discuss further in Chapter 2, cash flow drives shareholder value, and economic profits drive the shareholder value that is created in excess of the capital invested in a company (or business).

WHAT'S REQUIRED TO EFFECTIVELY MANAGE SHAREHOLDER VALUE?

When you chip away all the stuff that doesn't work and lay to rest all the misconceptions, you are left with five core principles shared by the CEOs who have been able to sustain superior total shareholder returns over time:

1. ***Establish the right definition of winning and measure of success.***

   The executives at shareholder-value-managed companies believe that their ultimate objective is to deliver superior returns for their stockholders over time. They define winning as (a) delivering higher returns for their shareholders relative to their industry peers by (b) delivering consistently greater cash flow and economic profit growth than their peers. While these executives acknowledge the importance of revenue growth, market share, earnings per share, and return on capital, they understand that focusing on any of these measures in isolation can lead to sub-optimal shareholder value creation.

2. ***Capitalize on the fact that shareholder value is always highly concentrated.***

   The executives at shareholder-value-managed companies know that economic profits and shareholder value contribution are always highly concentrated in every market and market segment. These executives capitalize on the tremendous performance leverage that this concentration offers. They make sure their managers are developing strategies and allocating resources in ways that increase their share of economic profits in each market where they participate, while letting their less informed competition pursue growth in the economically unprofitable segments of these markets.

   These CEOs constantly remind their management teams to eliminate economic losses and redirect investment to accelerate the growth of economically profitable business segments. Through this redirection and a renewed focus, these companies succeed in establishing and sustaining a reinvestment advantage that is difficult for competitors to match.

3. *Actively pursue the highest value-at-stake opportunities.*

   These chief executives behave like activist investors, continuously seeking out and then concentrating on the issues and opportunities that will have the greatest impact on their company's economic profit growth and shareholder value. They recognize that only a handful of strategic decisions will ultimately determine whether their company outperforms or underperforms its peers. These executives do not become overwhelmed by an endless list of tactical initiatives that diffuse their focus and spread resources so thin that they don't have much impact.

4. *Deploy differentiated strategies, and differentially allocate resources against those strategies.*

   Executives at value-managed companies understand that economically profitable growth and superior shareholder returns are the result of economically differentiated strategies and the differential allocation of resources. As a result, they do not attempt to copy "best-demonstrated practices." Rather, they develop and deploy business models that uniquely satisfy the needs of profitable customers more effectively than their competitors, thereby capturing a disproportionate share of the available profits in the markets they serve. They ask the uncomfortable questions, challenge historical assumptions, and accept—even embrace—the fact that creative destruction is constantly at work in every market and that shareholder resources must continually flow toward value-creating opportunities and away from value-consuming ones. They know that they must proactively manage this reallocation of resources—or the capital markets will do it for them.

5. *Build the organizational conditions and capabilities to manage shareholder value.*

These executives appreciate that one of their primary responsibilities is to instill throughout the company a set of beliefs and behaviors that are aligned with the long-term interests of the company's shareholders. These CEOs recognize that superior performance is ultimately the result of an organizational advantage. They create this advantage by building the organizational conditions and capabilities that encourage their managers to think and act like owners.

Figure 1.2 summarizes the contrasting characteristics of typical companies and value-managed companies. The table both serves as a quick review of the five principles discussed in the preceding pages and gives you a chance to consider how your organization compares.

Beliefs and Behaviors	Typical Company	Shareholder-Value-Managed Company	Your Company
1. Winning and Measure of Success	• *Goal:* Grow shareholder value • *Performance measures:* Multiple and sometimes competing financial and strategic targets (e.g., share gains, EPS growth, return on capital, etc.)	• *Goal:* Maximize shareholder value • *Performance measures:* Overriding focus on growing economic profit; other performance measures are subordinate	?
2. Market Attractiveness and Competitive Advantage	• *Attractive markets:* Large and growing volume and/or revenues • *Competitive advantage:* Leading market share	• *Attractive markets:* Large and growing economic profit pools • *Competitive advantage:* Leading share of economic profits	?

Figure 1.2: How Shareholder-Value-Managed Companies Are Different

continues on next page

continued from previous page

Beliefs and Behaviors	Typical Company	Shareholder-Value-Managed Company	Your Company
3. Management Agenda and Focus	• Broad statements of strategic direction • Long list of tactical initiatives	• Specific definition of where and how to compete • Short list of highest value-at-stake opportunities	?
4. Strategies and Resource Allocation Decisions	• Match "best-demonstrated practices" • Reduce risk through diversification • Egalitarian allocation of resources, in proportion to current size of business	• Adopt differentiated strategies • Reduce risk through differentiation and competitive advantage • Differential allocation of resources to value-creating strategies and away from value-consuming strategies	?
5. Organizational Conditions and Capabilities	• Budgets drive strategic and resource decisions • Business boundaries designed to achieve functional economies of scale • Incentives tied to revenue and operating margin growth	• Strategies drive budgets and resource allocation decisions • Business boundaries designed to maximize transparency and accountability for economic profits • Incentives tied to economic profit growth	?
Outcomes	• Declining differentiation and loss of pricing power • Lower return on capital, declining P/E ratio, and declining shareholder returns • Deteriorating reinvestment potential	• Improved differentiation and pricing power • Increased return on capital and shareholder returns • Increased reinvestment potential and competitive advantage	?

YOU ALREADY KNOW THIS . . . BUT DOES EVERYONE ELSE IN YOUR ORGANIZATION BEHAVE ACCORDINGLY?

Often, when we describe what we have learned from working with CEOs who have consistently delivered superior shareholder value and go on to sketch out the five principles underlying their success, our clients say something like, "I knew all this. I may not have put it in exactly those words, but those are exactly my views."

That doesn't surprise us. As we've said, we have only met a few CEOs who do not believe their ultimate goal is to increase shareholder value. So we agree with you: you do get it. And if you were making every decision in your organization, you would make just about all of them correctly.

But you have hundreds if not thousands of managers in your organization who are making decisions that have at least some impact on shareholder value, and they don't get it as well as you do.

Travis Engen, who ran ITT Industries and later Alcan, explains the challenge well: "In my life, the difficult problem hasn't been figuring out what to do; it has always been getting other people to reach similar, or at least congruent, conclusions. As I've matured through my business career, I've gone from basically being an engineer to being a people engineer, figuring out how to get people interested, motivated, excited, and passionate about working collaboratively on things that are important, on improving total shareholder returns."

This book is intended to be a resource for doing just that—getting all your managers to think and act like owners.

SUMMARY AND KEY TAKEAWAYS

▸ Internal management misconceptions (about what drives shareholder value and how to manage its growth), not external competition, are the most significant impediment to improving shareholder returns.

▸ Overcoming these misconceptions, and instilling the organizational beliefs and conditions that encourage the right behaviors, distinguishes CEOs who have been able to effectively manage shareholder value growth from those who have not.

▸ While every organization is different, and CEOs need to tailor their approach and their leadership to the specific needs of their companies, we have found that the following five core beliefs distinguish the successful efforts from the less successful ones:

1. Winning is ultimately defined by delivering higher sustainable shareholder returns than your competition. In order to win, you must do a better job of creating and capturing customer value for your shareholders. If you do, you will realize higher levels of cash flow and economic profit growth than your competition.

2. Shareholder value contribution and growth are *always* highly concentrated. This concentration offers a tremendous opportunity to better focus your strategies and resources on capturing a disproportionate share of economic profits in every served market, thereby achieving a reinvestment advantage that is difficult for competitors to replicate.

3. There are only a handful of opportunities to *significantly* impact the economic profit growth of an entire corporation; keeping time and resources focused on those opportunities is the way to run a company.

4. Good performance is the result of doing things better. Superior performance is the result of doing things differently. In order to maximize shareholder value, businesses must develop differentiated strategies and differentially allocate resources.

5. Shareholder value is impacted by the daily decisions and actions of hundreds of managers. Adopting the beliefs and organizational conditions that align these decisions and actions with shareholder interests is the only way to sustain superior performance.

CHAPTER 2

Redefining Winning and the Measure of Success

"Every company needs a governing objective—a driving force by which it measures its ultimate performance."

—Sir Brian Pitman, former Chairman and CEO, Lloyds TSB

- To be successful, every organization needs a clear definition of winning and measure of success.

- The ultimate measure of success for any publicly traded corporation is delivering superior shareholder returns over time, relative to its peers. All stakeholders benefit when shareholder value improves.

- In order to achieve superior shareholder returns, companies must do a better job than their competition at creating customer value and then capturing a portion of that value for the company's shareholders.

- The best internal measure of shareholder value contribution is the cash flow and economic profit that a business generates over time.

All leaders of successful organizations have one thing in common: they have established an unambiguous and singular definition of winning. Their organizations are absolutely clear on what they are trying to achieve and how they will ultimately measure success. When you think about it, it would be impossible for an entire organization to keep rowing in the same direction without such clarity. It is just not feasible for a single person or group of people, no matter where they are in the organization, to make a consistent set of decisions and trade-offs over time without a consistent definition of winning, and without a consistent measure of success and criterion for making strategic and resource allocation decisions.

Value-managed companies make their definition of winning explicitly clear. As Roberto Goizueta famously stated in Coca-Cola's 1994 annual report: "We are never confused about why we exist. Although volume growth, earnings, returns [on capital], and cash flow are important, our people understand that those measurements are all simply the means to the long-term end of creating value for our shareowners. Management's primary objective is to create as much value as possible for our shareowners." That focus paid off. Under Goizueta's leadership from 1981 to 1997, Coca-Cola delivered a compounded annual total shareholder return of 27 percent.

Warren Buffett, one of the world's greatest creators of shareholder value, a director of Coca-Cola, and Chairman and Chief Executive of Berkshire Hathaway, agrees. In describing the governing objective for Berkshire, he states, "Our long-term goal is to maximize the annual rate of gain in intrinsic business value. We define intrinsic value as the discounted value of the cash that can be taken out of a business during its remaining life . . . . Intrinsic value is all-important and is the only logical way to evaluate the relative attractiveness of investments and businesses."[4]

As Don Knauss, Chairman and CEO of Clorox, says, "Shareholder value establishes a True North. The potential impact on shareholder value is the ultimate criterion by which all key decisions are made."

This clear definition of winning is in sharp contrast to statements by other corporate leaders, such as John Smale, the former Chairman of General Motors, who believed that "winning" is defined by the overall size, revenue growth, and longevity of the corporation. In his words, "A corporation is a human, living enterprise. It is not just a bunch of assets. The obligation of management is to perpetuate the corporation, and that precedes their obligation to shareholders." True to his definition of winning, during Mr. Smale's tenure, GM's sales grew about 8 percent faster than those of its peers. However, GM's shareholder returns significantly lagged behind those of its competitors. Over time, GM's definition of winning led to a predicable outcome: not only were GM shareholders poorly served, but so were its employees, suppliers, and the communities in which it operated. The only way GM management was able to "perpetuate the corporation" was to be bailed out by the U.S. government at enormous expense to bondholders and the U.S. taxpayers.

The Gillette Company Story

To consider just how important the right definition of winning is, let's look at a case example.

Gillette is an iconic brand that holds a leading share of the global razors and blades business. For many years it was the darling of Wall Street, meeting quarterly earnings-per-share targets and delivering impressive shareholder returns. Over time, however, "playing the EPS game" eventually caught up with the company. While focused on short-term financial outcomes, management lost sight of the underlying changes in market economics, as consumers began switching to disposable blades sold by Gillette's competitors and the retail trade continued to consolidate and demand lower prices. Both of these changes had a negative impact on Gillette's cash flow and economic profit growth.

As time went on, management began taking short-cuts to meet quarterly earnings expectations, reducing R&D and promotion costs, loading the trade with dis-counted products at the end of each quarter, and making overpriced acquisitions to boost earnings.

Ultimately, Gillette's management could no longer disguise the company's declining performance. (See Figure 2.1.) The company began missing its externally

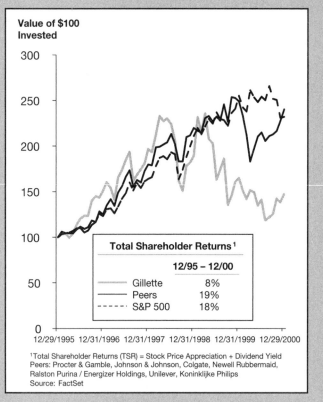

Value of $100 Invested

Total Shareholder Returns[1]	
12/95 – 12/00	
Gillette	8%
Peers	19%
S&P 500	18%

12/29/1995 12/31/1996 12/31/1997 12/31/1998 12/31/1999 12/29/2000

[1]Total Shareholder Returns (TSR) = Stock Price Appreciation + Dividend Yield
Peers: Procter & Gamble, Johnson & Johnson, Colgate, Newell Rubbermaid,
Ralston Purina / Energizer Holdings, Unilever, Koninklijke Philips
Source: FactSet

Figure 2.1: Gillette's Shareholder Returns Compared with Its Competitors

communicated earnings targets and shareholder value declined significantly.

In 2001, when Jim Kilts took over as Chief Executive of Gillette, he changed the definition of winning and the company's internal measure of success. Prior management had defined winning as meeting the company's guidance on quarterly and annual earnings forecasts. In his first month at Gillette, Kilts announced, "We are no longer playing the 'earnings game'; instead, we are going to start playing the 'value game.' Our goal is to deliver superior shareholder returns relative to our peers."

Kilts stopped providing analysts with earnings forecasts and began measuring each of Gillette's five global business units on their earnings minus a charge for the capital employed to generate those earnings. The company called this measure "economic profits." Kilts told his managers, "We are going to start measuring success not just by market share and earnings but by the economic profits that each business generates." Kilts required each Gillette business team to undertake a systematic strategic evaluation of where and why they were generating economic profits and losses and identify how to fix the economically unprofitable businesses and increase the growth of the economically profitable businesses.

As we will explain in later pages, the transformation that began with this redefinition of winning and measure of success ultimately led to a 225-percent increase in Gillette's shareholder value over a four-year period. This created an additional $26 billion in capital gains and dividends for those who invested in Gillette instead of an index of its peer companies. (See Figure 2.2.)

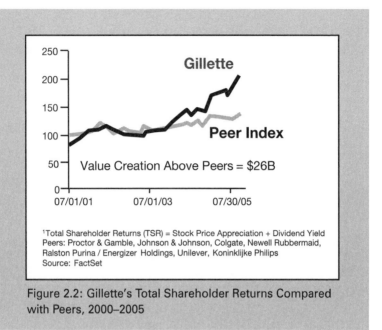

Figure 2.2: Gillette's Total Shareholder Returns Compared with Peers, 2000–2005

EXTERNAL MEASURE OF SUCCESS

Executives at companies that define winning in terms of shareholder returns compare the compounded annual returns their company delivers to their shareholders—measured by the appreciation in stock price plus dividend yield—with those of their competitors. They use this measure because it normalizes for factors that might impact all competitors in an industry and focuses attention on the company's relative performance within its industry.

Over time, this comparison is the ultimate measure of how well management has done, relative to its competition, in both creating customer value and capturing that value for the company's shareholders.

The Tortoise and the Hare

Why should top quartile performance be the goal? Why not try to be the top-performing company year after year?

The CEOs who are best at producing superior shareholder returns say, intriguingly, that the best way to end up being number one over time is to aim to be in the top 25 percent year after year.

"I did a study about this back when I was in grad school [at the University of Chicago]," Jim Kilts said, "and it turns out that those companies that are always in the top 25 percent in terms of total shareholder returns end up being number one when you look at the results for a ten-year period."

Kelly King, Chairman and CEO of BB&T, has seen the same thing from the opposite end of the telescope: "What I've learned in watching other businesses over the years, and watching our own performance, is that if your goal is always to be number one every year, then you almost never make it. When a business always tries to be number one, it causes them to drift down the slippery slope of short-term focus. They know they need to do some things for the long term—upgrade the IT systems, seriously invest in training and leadership development—but they don't because they have been number one for five years in a row and they don't want to slip.

"Well, by not doing the things they need to do, eventually they slip and, in fact, fall off the road.

"I've seen this happen in our company. We divided our company into what we refer to as regional banks. They're not legal entities, but they are specific geographic areas that a president runs with his own senior leadership team. I evaluate each region relative to one another. We compare them on quality, profitability, and growth, in that order. And what I found is that the regions that tried to knock home runs every time would be number one for a year, or maybe two, and then they'd go to number ten or fifteen or twenty, or fall to the bottom of the list. When you went in and examined why, you'd find they were short-terming.

"And then I observed our other presidents who didn't have quite as big egos, who were more focused on running their businesses. They never focused on trying to be number one. They focused on trying to be in the top quartile, typically, in everything. And so what you find out is, if someone is shooting for the top quartile in quality, profitability, and growth on a consistent basis, they end up being consistently near the top year after year, and in the long term as well."

Kilts acknowledges, "It can take the outside world a while to catch up to why this approach makes sense.

"I am so tired of people saying I am not aspirational enough when I say our goal is to be in the top quartile year after year. I tell them I am very aspirational. I want to do relatively better than the competition over a longer period of time—over a three-, five-, or ten-year period.

"I avoid the yo-yo effects my competitors go through. This year they are number one. Next year they are the worst. What I want is consistency of results based on innovation, efficiency of cost, and productivity management. I want to be at the top of my industry over a period of time."

INTERNAL MEASURE OF SUCCESS

While delivering superior shareholder returns should be the governing objective of any publicly traded corporation, it can be a difficult goal to relate to if you are a line manager. While share price performance is of interest, especially to those who participate in stock-ownership plans, it is difficult for most employees to understand how their actions impact that price. That's why, in addition to tracking relative shareholder returns, companies must also have a consistent internal measure of success that is directly related to shareholder value.

After all, left to their own devices, everyone could have their own measures of success. The marketing department could measure success in terms of market share, only to end up capturing unprofitable volume. The manufacturing organization could measure success in terms of production rates, only to produce a greater percentage of defective products. The quality department could measure success in terms of the percentage of error-free production, only to find that the investment required to realize the next increment of quality is not valued by the customer.

While there are any number of measures of success that are important in tracking performance, there is only one measure that is directly related to shareholder value. That measure is economic profit.

What Is Economic Profit?

Economic profit is the true profitability of a company (or business). It is equal to the revenue generated by a company (or business) minus all the costs, including the cost of the capital that is required to generate that revenue.

While traditional measures of corporate profit, such as net income, consider interest expense (the cost of debt) to be an expense, the cost of the equity capital employed in the company is not reflected as an expense.

The situation is even worse at the business unit level. Traditional measures of business unit profitability, such as operating profit, not only exclude the cost of equity capital, they exclude interest expense and other corporate or shared-service costs that support the operation of the business unit.

What is the problem with not considering all expenses? Without a true understanding of profitability, management can make bad strategic and resource allocation decisions that consume shareholder value.

When the full economic costs of operating a business are not included in the calculation of business profitability, management is flying blind, unable to distinguish between revenue that is contributing to shareholder value and revenue that is consuming shareholder value.

What's Wrong with This Picture?

One of the many oddities of Generally Accepted Accounting Principles (GAAP) is that while interest expense (the cost of debt capital) is subtracted from operating earnings when calculating the net income of a business, the cost of the really expensive capital, equity capital, is not considered.

To see how big a difference that can make, let's look at one fictional company, Widgetmaster, which has earnings per share of $1.20.

Reflected in its net income was $375 million in interest expense on their debt, impacting EPS by $0.75 a share. If the company had recognized that it also needed to provide a return to shareholders on the $7.5 billion of equity capital invested in the business—say something modest, like 10 percent—then an additional charge of $750 million, or $1.50 a share, should have been subtracted from EPS as well.

This would have driven the EPS from its reported value of $1.20 to a *loss* of $0.30 a share. (See Figure 2.3.)

Impact of the Cost of Capital

	$MM	$/Share
Revenue	10,000	20.00
Operating Income	1,275	2.55
Interest Expense	375	0.75
Profit Before Tax	900	1.80
Taxes	300	0.60
Net Income	600	1.20
Equity Charge (@10%)	750	1.50
Economic Profit	-150	-0.30

Figure 2.3: Impact of the Cost of Capital on Earnings

CASH FLOW, ECONOMIC PROFIT, AND SHAREHOLDER VALUE

The discounted present value of the future economic profits is equal to the value of a company (or business) in excess of the capital that has been invested in the business. If a company is to sustain a market value in excess of its book value (i.e., market to book ratio greater than 1.0), investors must expect the company to generate economic profits. (See Figure 2.4.)

So how well do economic profit expectations correlate with a company's stock price and shareholder value creation? Figure 2.5 plots the correlation of the stock price of all S&P 500 companies with the discounted value of consensus forecasts of each company's future economic profit plus book equity per share. As you can see, there is a tight correlation between the actual and forecasted values of most S&P 500 companies. This strong correlation has existed for at least the last six decades.

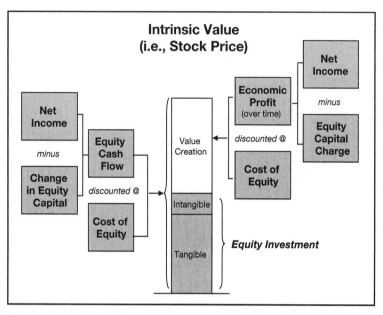

Figure 2.4: Financial Determinants of Shareholder Value

"Yes," you might say, "but there is also a close correlation between earnings growth and shareholder returns."

However, as Figure 2.6 shows, there actually is not. There is also little correlation between a company's earnings growth and its price to earnings ratio. This is not because earnings are not important. After all, GAAP earnings are a major contributor to cash flow, but so too is the amount of GAAP earnings that are reinvested in the company and the returns realized on that investment.

A company that generates the same amount of earnings growth with less capital produces more cash flow for dividends or new investments and therefore is worth more to its shareholders than a company that must reinvest a larger percentage of its earnings to sustain the existing business.

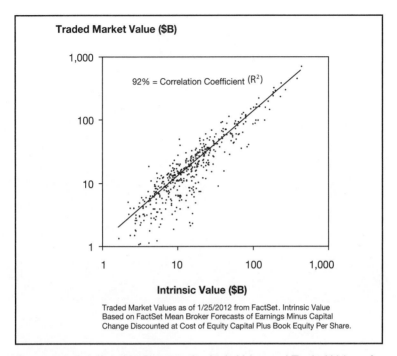

Traded Market Value ($B)

92% = Correlation Coefficient (R^2)

Intrinsic Value ($B)

Traded Market Values as of 1/25/2012 from FactSet. Intrinsic Value
Based on FactSet Mean Broker Forecasts of Earnings Minus Capital
Change Discounted at Cost of Equity Capital Plus Book Equity Per Share.

Figure 2.5: Relationship Between Intrinsic Value and Traded Value of
S&P 500 Companies

In summary, there is a tight correlation between the cash flow
and economic profit growth a company is able to generate and the
shareholder value of that company. Believing that earnings growth
alone drives shareholder value is one of the most prevalent management misconceptions. As you will read, this fundamental miscon-
ception can compound strategic and resource allocation mistakes
and limit the shareholder value growth of a company.

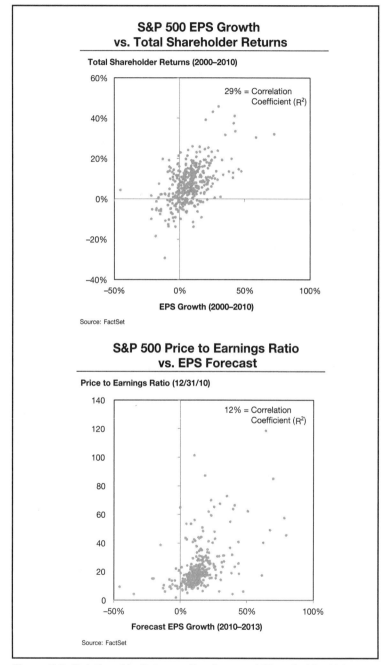

Figure 2.6: Relationship Between Earnings and Shareholder Value

SUMMING UP THE IMPORTANT YARDSTICKS

In summary, there are three yardsticks that are essential to effectively measure and manage shareholder value performance:

1. **Economic Profit (EP)**, which is the earnings generated by a company (or business), minus a charge for the capital employed to generate those earnings. EP is a single period measure of the true profitability from the shareholder's perspective.

> "Creating economic profit is the single most important driver of the stock price of the Coca-Cola Company."
> —Roberto Goizueta, former Chairman and CEO, the Coca-Cola Company

2. **Intrinsic Shareholder Value**, which is the discounted value of future cash flow generated by the company (or business). The discounted value of economic profits is equal to that portion of intrinsic value in excess of the capital invested in the company (or business). The discounted value of expected economic profits is the best internal measure of shareholder value creation and therefore the best criterion to use for choosing between strategic and resource allocation alternatives.

> "We define intrinsic value as the discounted value of the cash that can be taken out of a business during its remaining life. Despite its fuzziness . . .
> intrinsic value is all-important and is the only logical way to evaluate the relative attractiveness of investments and businesses."
> —Warren Buffett, Chairman and CEO, Berkshire Hathaway

3. **Total Shareholder Returns (TSR)**, which is the stock price appreciation plus dividend yield generated by a company over a given period of time. This is the ultimate measure of success and the most objective gauge of how well management is doing for its shareholders.

> "Maximizing shareholder value—by dividend increases and by share price appreciation—remains our governing objective."
> —Sir Brian Pitman, former Chairman and CEO, Lloyds TSB

WHERE DO MOST COMPANIES GO WRONG?

As previously stated, in order to achieve and sustain superior shareholder performance, companies must do a better job than their competitors at delivering value to customers and capturing a portion of that value for the company's shareholders. Yet most companies do a poor job of measuring and managing this linkage between the customer and capital markets. They either define winning in terms of customer market results, like market share, or they define winning in financial terms that are not directly tied to capital market performance, like earnings per share.

The Problem with Only Focusing on Market Share

The common, but misplaced, belief is that winning is entirely defined in the customer markets. Management teams assume that market share leadership always results in advantaged consumer awareness, better trade leverage, and superior economies of scale that naturally lead to superior financial results and shareholder value growth.

And yet, it is often the most differentiated competitor, not the competitor with the largest share position, that garners the greatest consumer attention, commands the greatest power over the trade, and is able to achieve higher utilization rates that more than offset any scale disadvantage.

As an example, consider Apple's success in the mobile phone market. While others were competing for leading share of handsets, Apple pursued a differentiated business model. It provided a unique but more costly product, initially sold only through a single telecom provider (AT&T), in exchange for a much larger share of the activation fees. Despite lower market share than its competitors, Apple began to earn much higher economic profits, profits that were reinvested to build out its own retail network and a complementary "ecosystem" of related services that further enhanced the value of its offer. Despite its late entry into the handset market, in four years Apple was able to capture over 50 percent of all industry economic profits with less than a 10 percent share of handset volume. As a result, Apple delivered total shareholder returns over 20 percentage points higher than the industry average. (See Figures 2.7 and 2.8.)

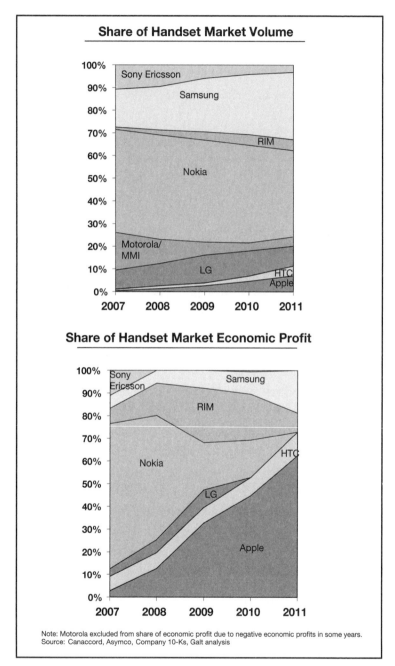

Figure 2.7: Handset-Provider Share of Handset Volume and Economic Profit

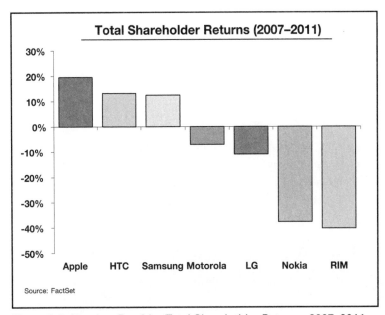

Figure 2.8: Handset Provider Total Shareholder Returns, 2007–2011

The Problem with Only Focusing on Earnings Growth

Equally disastrous is a focus on earnings growth without a commensurate focus on the investment required to generate those earnings.

Managers assume that increased earnings per share will translate into a higher stock price. They assume that a higher EPS will be multiplied by a static price/earnings ratio. But what is not fully appreciated is that P/E multiples are affected by the company's return on capital and its profitable growth prospects. If investments in earnings growth lead to declining returns on capital, then P/E multiples will fall, and that growth will contribute little—if at all—to share price appreciation.

Blind Pursuit of Earnings Growth: The U.S. Banking Industry

An incorrect definition of winning and the wrong measure of performance can be disastrous. The U.S. banking industry serves as a case in point.

Between 1995 and 2006, more than 70 percent of the industry's GAAP reported net income growth came from increased loan originations, especially in the commercial and residential real estate markets.

As competition for loan originations intensified, pricing and credit quality decreased to the point where new loans were not generating enough earnings to offset the cost of the capital required to support the increased loan balances.

The result? As early as 2003, the average mortgage was consuming shareholder value. However, Wall Street analysts and many bank CEOs continued to encourage growth in mortgage originations in order to drive earnings per share (EPS) higher.

Had bank executives been paying more attention to the capital required to generate those earnings, they would have recognized that the average retail and commercial real estate loan was economically unprofitable. (See Figure 2.9.)

As is the case with all economically unprofitable investments, investors eventually learned of the sinkhole that had been created. That happened when defaults began accelerating in 2007. The consequences of this mistake, for the most aggressive banks and mortgage originators and the industry as a whole, are now ancient history.

No financial institution was spared in the aftermath of the industry implosion. But banks such as BB&T that were

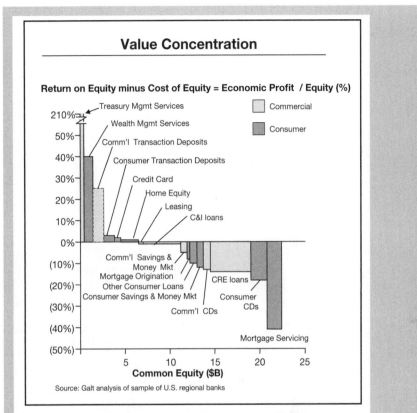

Figure 2.9: 2004 to 2006 Average Economic Profit Concentration at a Typical U.S. Regional Bank

Note: In Figure 2.9, the economic profit generated by each product segment is represented by the area of the corresponding rectangle, determined by multiplying the height of each bar (the amount of economic profit generated per dollar of equity investment) by the width of each bar (the amount of equity capital invested in the product segment).

pursuing economic profitability, not EPS growth, have performed much better than their competition.

As Kelly King, CEO of BB&T, explains, once you do an analysis to determine where an organization is actually generating economic profits, it can result in a radical change in the way you do business.

"I would say the implications of this analysis were initially relatively difficult to accept, because it challenged some fundamental beliefs," King says. "For example, one of the things we always assumed was that we make basically all of our money in lending and that we're really good lenders. What the economic profit analysis did was just completely flip that. It showed that for most of the decade deposits were generating a lot more economic profit than loans, and by the way, we were not doing a good job at all in terms of producing deposits.

"We had all these insurance customers and wealth management customers, but we were focusing on selling them insurance or making them loans. Making them loans and selling them insurance is fine, but guess what? It didn't produce a lot of economic profit. As a result of this analysis, we were able to redirect our efforts to extend our relationships and secure more of our customers' deposits. As a result, we produced a ton of economic profit growth."

Don't Assume Better Measures Alone Will Produce Better Results

Before concluding this chapter, we want to offer a note of caution: many companies incorrectly assume that all that is needed to better manage shareholder value is to tie management compensation to a performance measure, like economic profit, that is more closely aligned with shareholder value. However, this assumption has proven to be misplaced, as evidenced by the mixed performance of companies that have adopted measures like EVA™[5] (an equivalent measure to economic profit) but done little else to change the way their company is managed. (See Figure 2.10.)

Chief executives who have actually delivered superior shareholder value growth appreciate the difference between *measuring* and *managing* shareholder value. They realize that they not only need to create the incentive to improve economic profit growth but also the ability. Creating the ability to manage economic profit and shareholder value growth is the topic of the remainder of this book.

Sample EVA™ Companies			Performance Post EVA™ Adoption	
Ticker	Company	Mkt Cap ($B)	5 Year TSR	10 Year TSR
PG	Procter & Gamble Co.	181.7	3.6%	8.0%
T	AT&T Inc.	179.7	2.1%	2.6%
LLY	Eli Lilly & Co.	46.5	0.3%	-2.7%
BBY	Best Buy Co. Inc.	8.8	-12.5%	-2.4%
S	Sprint Nextel Corp.	7.0	-34.1%	-17.5%
EFX	Equifax	4.7	-0.1%	5.5%
WHR	Whirlpool Corp.	4.1	-8.1%	-1.8%
SPW	SPX Corp.	3.4	1.2%	0.1%
SMG	Scotts Miracle-Gro Co.	2.9	2.7%	9.7%
TDW	Tidewater Inc.	2.8	2.3%	5.7%
RRD	R.R. Donnelley & Sons Co.	2.2	-11.9%	-2.8%
OLN	Olin Corp.	1.7	8.2%	6.6%
HSC	Harsco Corp.	1.6	-9.5%	4.3%
MTW	Manitowoc	1.5	-20.3%	2.4%
CRUS	Cirrus Logic Inc.	1.3	18.2%	1.8%
MLHR	Herman Miller Inc.	1.2	-11.8%	-1.5%
BGG	Briggs & Stratton Corp.	0.9	-7.3%	-0.2%
	EVA™ Measurement Companies		**2.7%**	**4.0%**
	Industry Peer Group Averages		**3.0%**	**4.2%**
	Average Difference		**-0.4%**	**-0.2%**

Note: Total Shareholder Returns ending 12/30/2011

Source: EVA™ companies from Stern Stewart Research and company annual filings; financial results from FactSet

Figure 2.10: Total Shareholder Returns of sample EVA™ Companies

SUMMARY AND KEY TAKEAWAYS

▸ All good leaders understand that no group of individuals can be aligned unless there is a common definition of winning and measure of success.

▸ Companies that are effectively managed for shareholder value growth define winning as outperforming their peers in total shareholder returns over time. They recognize that in order to deliver superior shareholder returns, their company must do a better job than its competition at both (1) creating customer value and (2) capturing the optimal portion of that value for the company's shareholders.

▸ These leaders recognize that earnings growth alone is not sufficient to create shareholder value. While there are several important internal measures of performance, there is only one measure that defines success in both the customer and capital markets—the company's share of economic profits. They measure the success of their businesses by the economic profit *growth* that those businesses generate.

▸ Successful leaders recognize that improved measurements alone will not deliver improved results. They know that in order to deliver superior shareholder returns, managers must have both the incentive and the ability to deliver superior economic profit growth.

CHAPTER 3
Why Shareholder Value Is Always Highly Concentrated

. . . .

"Most companies perform at only about half their potential
to create shareholder value. Unprofitable customers and
unprofitable markets are some of the most difficult things
to get people to face up to."

—Sir Brian Pitman, former Chairman and CEO, Lloyds TSB

. . . .

- Shareholder value _is always_ highly concentrated because of differences in market economics and competitive position.

- In many corporations, less than 40 percent of employed capital is generating more than 100 percent of the company's stock price, while 25 to 35 percent of employed capital is actually destroying shareholder value. This concentration offers enormous potential to improve shareholder value.

- Most companies do not recognize this concentration because their management reports do not break down economic profits by business and business segment. However, this gap can be quickly overcome without overhauling the reporting system.

- Management can unlock significant shareholder value by better focusing its strategies and resources on growing economically profitable segments while fixing or withdrawing resources from economically unprofitable ones.

We all remember the famous quote from John Wanamaker, the man who created some of the first department stores on the East Coast: "Half the money you spend on advertising is wasted; the trouble is that you don't know which half."

Unfortunately, for most CEOs, the same statement applies to the resources (both human and capital) that are invested across their company.

In many Fortune 500 companies, less than 40 percent of the capital employed in the corporation is generating over 100 percent of the company's shareholder value, while 25 to 35 percent of the employed capital is destroying shareholder value.

Most executives simply don't believe that statement. And why should they, when they have spent their entire careers looking at management reports of operating profits instead of economic profits? Typical management accounting systems provide neither a complete view of profitability nor a granular enough view of business segment economics.

And yet, economic profits and shareholder value contribution are *always* concentrated by market, by company, by business, and by business segment (i.e., by product, customer, channel, etc.).

Why? Because of differences in market conditions (such as intensity of competition, threat of entry, supplier power, and customer power) that impact average market economics. And because of differences in the competitive position of businesses participating in that market.

This concentration of economic profits is the reason there is such enormous potential to improve the shareholder value of most corporations.

DIFFERENCES IN MARKET ECONOMICS

To see just how much economic profitability can vary, let's begin by taking a look across the entire economy. From 2006 to 2010, the average return on equity of the S&P 500 was approximately 4 percentage points greater than the average cost of equity. However, this spread between the returns on equity and the cost of equity varied significantly by industry. Approximately one-third of the total equity capital invested in the S&P 500 generated no economic profits over this five-year time frame. (See Figure 3.1.)

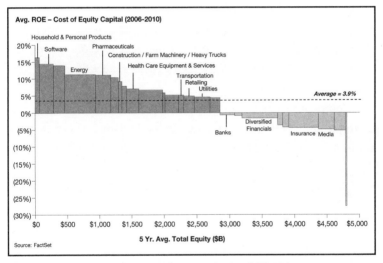

Figure 3.1: Shareholder Value Creation in the S&P 500

Note: In the figure above, the horizontal axis shows the average amount of shareholder equity (book value) that was employed in the various S&P 500 industries. On the vertical axis is the average return on equity, above the cost of equity, that was generated by each industry. The area within each industry rectangle (the amount of equity capital multiplied by the average return on equity minus the cost of equity) represents the average annual economic profit that was generated by each industry from 2006 to 2010.

DIFFERENCES IN COMPETITIVE POSITION

The spread between the return on capital and the cost of capital varies even more by competitor within a given industry. As an example, consider the construction, farm, mining machinery, and heavy truck market.

In 2008, Caterpillar was earning an average return on equity 26 percentage points higher than the company's cost of equity. If you multiply this return spread by the $7B of shareholder equity that was invested in Caterpillar, you find that the company generated $1.8B in economic profit that year. That was over 40 percent of the total economic profit generated by all major competitors in the construction, farming, mining, and machinery industry in 2008. (See Figure 3.2.) In capturing the leading share of economic profits in its industry, Caterpillar established a reinvestment advantage over its competition.

Competitors like Joy and Sany delivered higher returns on capital than Caterpillar, but on far less capital investment. Other competitors, like Volvo, Hitachi, and CNH, created no economic profit during this time period.

This same concentration of economic profits is demonstrated across all industries. In fact, *the biggest determinant of a company's economic profitability is not the industry in which it competes, but how it competes within that industry.*

DIFFERENCES IN SHAREHOLDER VALUE CONTRIBUTION WITHIN A COMPANY

Economic profitability and shareholder value contribution are also highly concentrated within a corporation. To illustrate, let's continue to use the example of Caterpillar. Based on Caterpillar's 2010 reported results, more than 100 percent of the company's economic

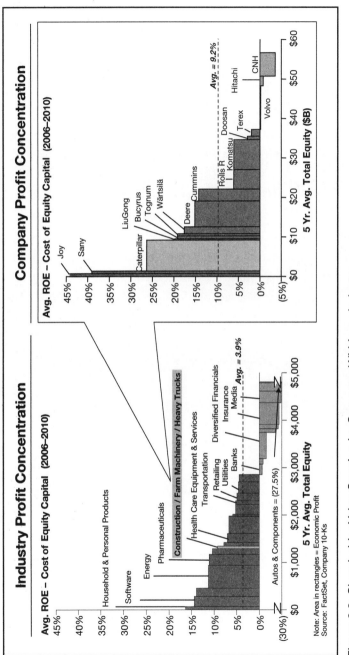

Figure 3.2: Shareholder-Value Creation by Company Within an Industry

profit was being generated by less than 30 percent of the company's total invested capital (i.e., debt plus equity capital). Meanwhile, over $28 billion of the total capital employed across the corporation was creating little to no shareholder value. Obviously, even the best companies have the potential to significantly improve economic profits and shareholder value.

DIFFERENCES IN SHAREHOLDER VALUE CONTRIBUTION WITHIN A BUSINESS UNIT

Within every business unit in a company, economic profits are also highly concentrated by product category, customer and channel segment, geographic region, and activity across the value chain.

This economic profit concentration is almost never apparent to managers, because as we previously mentioned, the accounting

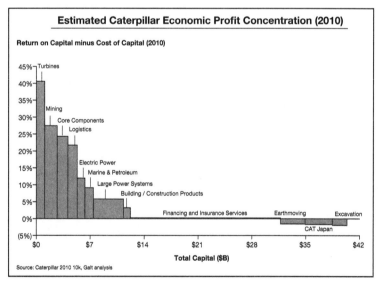

Figure 3.3: Caterpillar Profit Concentration, 2010

systems rarely allocate total expenses, including the cost of capital, to business segments.

In one sense, avoiding the trouble of allocating all costs and capital to each business and business segment is understandable. After all, allocation methodologies are always less than precise. However, in an effort to avoid false precision, management is often missing the strategic insights that a more granular understanding of economic profit provides.

Excuses, Excuses

There are three common excuses for not developing segment level measures of economic profitability:

- "We don't have the systems."
- "The accountants are not comfortable with the precision of the measures."
- "There are too many interdependencies to go to the trouble."

In the next few pages, Miles White, John Allison, Sir Brian Pitman, and Don Knauss help you understand why you should not let these excuses deter you. These CEOs will emphasize that the ability to measure economic profit at a granular segment level currently exists in all companies. Furthermore, they will emphasize that you can develop that information without investing tens or hundreds of millions of dollars and months of time upgrading your company's reporting systems. An Excel model and a few well-trained analysts will provide all the information that is needed to develop an initial understanding of this concentration and its strategic implications.

While your accounting team may challenge the precision of any particular allocation methodology, you will find that almost any rational approach will highlight the extreme concentrations of economic profitability that exist across and within all businesses.

Finally, while interdependencies between business segments must be considered, these interdependencies should be dimensioned and quantified. While some economically unprofitable products and services may be required to satisfy profitable customer needs, management must be willing to challenge the historical assumptions about the degree of unprofitability required to provide a compelling customer bundle, and even the type of customers a company should be pursuing.

As John Allison, the former Chairman and Chief Executive of BB&T, states, "It gets back to understanding where you really are making your money. Like most companies, we tended to know the answer to that question at the macro level. For example, at BB&T we knew commercial lending was a profitable business. But when we really dug into it, we found we just weren't making any money in small-business lending. Our delivery costs were just too high. Only then did we begin to focus on how to make that business segment more profitable while continuing to satisfy the needs of our customers."

Economically unprofitable businesses and business segments are a hidden cancer. They may be generating top-line growth and positive operating margins and, as a result, management may still be investing to grow them. However, with every dollar of investment, the return to shareholders is less than a dollar. These businesses are consuming shareholder value!

Sir Brian Pitman, former Chairman and Chief Executive of Lloyds TSB, understood all this perfectly. As he put it, "Maximizing value requires a focus on value to and value of customers. But you must recognize that not all customers are equal."

That statement raises a key point: do you know which customers create the most value and how to make them even more valuable?

And while you are sorting through your customer base to discover who your most valuable customers are, presumably your competitors are doing the same thing. So you want to segment your markets one level deeper than the competition. You want to go at least one layer further than they do in dissecting and analyzing your customers' needs, purchase patterns, and economics. That way, you can better understand how to profitably satisfy those needs.

There are three key benefits that come from developing a more granular understanding of your business. First, you are better able to identify and eliminate activities and investments that are destroying value. Second, you are better able to identify and act on segments of your business that are currently unprofitable but can be fixed. And third, you are better able to focus your resources on those aspects of your business that drive profitable differentiation. If you focus your resources on better satisfying profitable customers, you will outperform any competitor that is distributing their resources across an entire market.

DEVELOPING A GRANULAR UNDERSTANDING TO IMPROVE RESULTS

Understanding where and why economic profits are concentrated, and how that concentration is likely to change in the future, provides management with a tremendous advantage in deciding where to invest time, effort, and capital.

However, getting an organization to adopt that discipline can be challenging.

Miles White, of Abbott Labs, offers his perspective: "Once you make the commitment to understanding granularity, you need to keep at it. You've got to keep measuring the right things systemically.

You can't fall back into old practices. And there is a tendency to fall back into old practices. As management changes over time, especially if the managers did not go through the analysis process in the first place, it is not inculcated in them. They don't know as much. Their depth of learning and knowledge, at a real visceral level, isn't there. You can see this deteriorate over time just by the evolution of change in management and change in people who come into the division from other divisions or other companies. There's a real risk that you will go back to the way things were.

"In our case, we put in place a multi-year plan that had a lot of actions in it that were all driven toward achieving everything we'd learned in our analysis of the sources and drivers of economic profit growth. So that plan itself is a vehicle that keeps us focused on all the right points. We've shifted the locations of a lot of our manufacturing. We've outsourced parts of it. We've changed our service model. We've changed the way we measure profit and loss in the business. We've changed the way we incent salespeople, country managers, etc. And we track and measure our performance against the original projections and plans we put in place."

White also offers a cautionary note: "You don't want to eliminate things that have the potential to produce huge economic profit in the future just because they are not producing it now."

Unfortunately, Miles White's approach is the exception rather than the rule. As a consequence, most management teams do not appreciate just how concentrated economic profits are across their businesses and the markets they serve. As a result, they continue to blindly pursue growth in all market segments and fail to capitalize on the latent shareholder value improvement potential that exists across their companies.

How Long Do You Wait for a Turnaround?

Yes, of course you want to turn EP-losing divisions, customers, and products into profitable ones if you can. But you can't wait forever to see if the turnaround will happen. How long should you wait? Well, if the division or project in question is large enough, BB&T Chairman and CEO Kelly King suggests five years.

"It will vary, of course. But I think it is a good number," he says. "Here's an example: we started up a payroll business. We were going to compete with ADP. We had all these small-business clients. They needed payroll done. So, it was natural. And by the way, if we could get their payroll account, we could tie that to their 401(k), insurance, and everything else. It was a really good idea.

"So we tried to start a payroll division and we lost money. Then we tried a different approach and we lost money. After about five years we finally said, 'We can't do this.' In theory we can; in practice we can't. It was just hard to get people to switch to us.

"My business managers kept telling me that success was just around the corner—and they told me that up to the very day I pulled the plug. I finally said, 'Even if you turn the corner next year, you've just turned the corner. You're light years from where you'd have to be for it to be a meaningful enough business to stay in.'

"It was about five years from start to finish. Why didn't I end it sooner? Well, for one thing, they really did believe success was just around the corner. And obviously, by that point, we're already in the game. If I had known what I knew at the end, and I wasn't already in there, I wouldn't have gotten in. But I was already in it.

"And there are human beings involved. These are my employees, they are not just checkers pieces, and I have to worry about my employees as well as my shareholders. I've got to worry about both groups. I wanted to try to find a way to enhance what these folks were doing so that they could produce positive economic profit, so that it would be both good for the shareholders and the employees, as opposed to just cutting their heads off.

"Now, sometimes investors don't like that answer. I understand. And what I tell them is, 'Look, my job as CEO is to express as clearly to you as I can how I'm trying to shepherd the money you invested in us. You get to vote every day. If you don't like your investment, you can vote out today. I've been here thirty-nine years. This has been my life. So I don't vote every day. I'm not going anywhere. I take a longer-term view. You can take a short-term view. I understand and I respect that. But I'm taking a long-term view. If you're interested in short-term investments, I would recommend you not buy our stock.' I just tell them straight up.

"That said, five years is probably as long as I am going to give a major turnaround effort. If you have a business that is producing negative economic profit and you try for five years and you never get to positive, well, it's pretty clear that maybe somebody else will figure this out, but we can't. So we need to lose that business."

Identifying Profitable Growth Opportunities at Clorox

You may be thinking, "Yes, I agree; profitability does vary across and within all business units but, for the most part, all the business units in my company are quite profitable, even if I factor in the cost of capital. My biggest challenge is increasing growth. How is a more granular understanding of segment economics going to help my management teams do that?"

To answer that question, let's ask Don Knauss, CEO of Clorox.

"Clorox was a well-managed company when I got there," says Don, who became CEO in 2006. "You'd look at the portfolio and see that about 85 to 90 percent of our brands [including Clorox bleach, Armor All, Glad bags, Fresh Step cat litter, Hidden Valley, and KC Masterpiece dressings and sauces] generated exceptional economic profit margins, and these brands were number one or number two in their space. But the real problem was that we were in the fourth quartile when it came to revenue growth. Part of that issue was because the brands were being milked, and part was because we were participating in mature categories with lower growth. We weren't pushing to get into categories that had tailwinds. To improve shareholder value, do more than improve margins, we had to improve economic profit growth.

"One of the things I did after I arrived at Clorox was get the company focused on a few major trends: health and wellness, sustainability, affordable convenience, and the ethnic and multicultural shifts in the country and around the world. I said, 'Look, guys, these are the four trends we're going to focus on to improve profitable growth, and I am expecting every division, including Kingsford Charcoal, for example, to find a way to make itself relevant against one or all of those four trends, because they are enduring. And they're relevant around the globe.'"

Since Knauss delivered his edict, Kingsford has been one of Clorox's fastest-growing divisions. "It's really interesting how they figured it out," Knauss says. "It's an amazing story because when I got here, the brand was supposed to be dying because of the advent of gas grills. Who wants to grill with charcoal anymore?"

Here's what happened: "We did some research and found that families who eat together several times a week have better dynamics—less teenage drinking, less teenage pregnancy—than families who don't. So I said, 'Okay, that's the wellness side of health and wellness. You want to make the family even more robust—how can Kingsford play a role in that aspect of wellness? Well, we can be an anchor to meal solutions, especially on the weekend.'

"With that as the starting point, I said, 'We've got to make this brand a fifty-two-week brand, instead of a Memorial Day to Labor Day brand. We've got to make grilling acceptable throughout the year.'

"So first we created strong summer programs. And then we came up with the idea of tailgating at home. Once football season started, after Labor Day, we made a big push with retailers to create meal solutions where families and friends could get together and tailgate in their backyards instead of at the stadium. And it exploded the business. Retailers begin to say, 'I really want something to tie in with my meat in the butcher shop or the deli. I can tie the Kingsford promotion in with my condiments, my hot dog and hamburger buns.'

"We created these events every weekend around college football and pro football. And all of a sudden, Kingsford became not just a thirteen-week brand, but a thirty-five-week brand. It has been one of the fastest-growing brands over the past three years, with sales growing at an 8 percent compound rate."

Knauss goes on to point out, "Even the identification of economically unprofitable business segments can lead to new thinking and new profitable growth opportunities. Take the Glad business for example.

"Clorox acquired Glad in 1999. Then we created a joint venture with Procter & Gamble that drove some interesting stretchable technology for Glad Force-Flex and Odor Shield and for a couple of years that technology made Glad the darling of the company in terms of top-line growth. And if you had looked at only that, you would have thought Glad was doing fine across the board.

"But as we started digging into it, we said, 'Great, we are realizing overall growth, but parts of the business—like private label—are actually destroying value.' So we had to act.

"Our Glad private label business accounted for $300 million in revenue. We couldn't just lop it off. The stranded cost and the overhead left over would have been untenable. We couldn't really raise prices and there wasn't a way to add value to the basic bag. To a consumer, the basic bag is undifferentiated. The question became, how could we become the low-cost producer?

"We took advantage of some technology we were using on Force-Flex and Odor Shield bags to create the lightest bags possible that would still have acceptable performance. As a result, the business's economic profit margins turned positive, and we also dramatically increased top-line growth."

Knauss also highlights the need to understand channel as well as product segment economics. "One of the things we learned from developing an in-depth understanding of business segment economics was that we had been ignoring our traditional grocery business. The classic supermarket business had been declining in revenues year in and year out. Now it was down to about a third of our business because the grocers had been losing share to Walmart, Target, Costco, Sam's, and Dollar General and Family Dollar. And we had seen those channels really growing at the expense of the supermarkets.

"But as we dug into economic profit by channel, we realized that, yes, it was a third of our volume, but it was half of our economic profit. We said, 'Holy cow, we've been pulling investment out of grocery for years, shifting people into other channels like Walmart because they're growing fast on the top line.' But the fact is, groceries are by far the most economically profitable channel for us because they tend to carry a lot more of our SKUs, a lot more sizes than someone like Costco, who may carry one-fifth the SKUs we have in Kroger. And Costco is going to beat you up because there are fewer

SKUs, so they are going to want their pound of flesh if you want to be on the shelf.

"Once we really understood this, we said, 'Oh my God, we better start investing back in grocery.' And so over the next year, we added thirty to forty people and created a whole different regional team structure to go out and drive the grocery business."

WHERE DO COMPANIES GO WRONG?

The consequences of not developing a granular understanding of *where* and *why* economic profits are concentrated within your business and the markets you serve can be disastrous, as the following example of the cola wars in the United States will illustrate.

Competing for Share of Profits Versus Share of Volume: The U.S. Cola Wars

During Roberto Goizueta's tenure as chief executive, Coca-Cola was one of the best value-managed companies in the world. Coca-Cola consistently outperformed Pepsi, creating more customer value and capturing more of that value for Coca-Cola's shareholders. From 1981 until Goizueta's death in 1997, Coca-Cola's economic profits and shareholder value grew at a compounded annual growth rate of approximately 27 percent. In the North American market alone, Coca-Cola was able to capture well over 50 percent of the total economic profits produced by all competitors in the non-alcoholic beverage market. This economic profit leadership provided the company with the investment dollars needed to expand into adjacent beverage markets and grow internationally. (A more in-depth discussion of how Coca-Cola was able to achieve such success under Goizueta's leadership can be found in Chapter 7.)

However, after Goizueta's death, the company's new leadership lost focus on economic profits. The company stopped measuring economic profitability at the product, channel, and package level, and instead, began focusing on volume growth—at almost any cost. The company received an added push in this direction from Wall Street sell-side analysts, whose simplistic stock valuation models assumed all volume was equally profitable and therefore that all volume growth equated to shareholder value growth.

At the same time, under the leadership of then-Chairman Steven Reinemund, Pepsi began focusing on gaining share of the economic profits in each market and market segment. Pepsi management understood that the channels through which both carbonated and non-carbonated beverages were sold had a significant impact on profitability. More specifically, Pepsi management knew that economic profit per case was several times greater in the convenience retail and small "mom and pop" food outlets than it was in large grocery stores and national quick-service restaurants. (See Figure 3.4.)

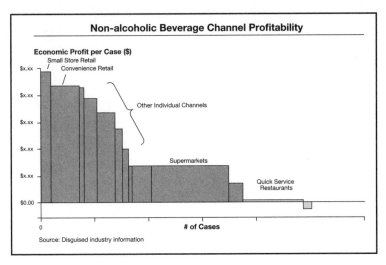

Figure 3.4: Non-alcoholic Beverage Channel Profitability

Based on a better understanding of segment economics, Pepsi began pursuing a deliberate strategy of gaining share in the most profitable channels. As a result, by the mid-2000s, Pepsi was able to reverse Coca-Cola's historical profit advantage and ended up capturing 60 percent of the total economic profits generated in the non-alcoholic beverage market in North America. Pepsi's total shareholder returns over this period exceeded those of Coca-Cola. (See Figure 3.5.)

Subsequently, under the leadership of Neville Isdell and Muhtar Kent, Coca-Cola has regained its understanding of and passion for growing the company's share of economic profits and has reversed these trends. However, several tens of billions of dollars' worth of Coca-Cola shareholder value was lost in the interim.

ONE LAST THOUGHT: REINVESTMENT ADVANTAGE

Economic profits are *always* highly concentrated. Those companies that are able to capture and maintain a leading share of economic profits establish a reinvestment advantage that is very difficult to match. This is why the best companies are able to deliver superior shareholder returns over an extended period of time.

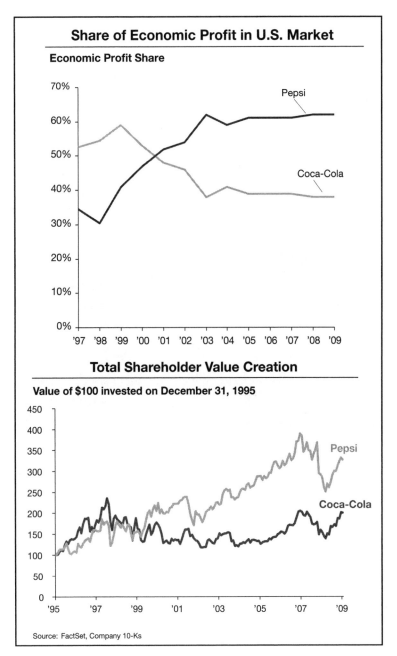

Figure 3.5: Coca-Cola and Pepsi Relative Shareholder-Value Creation

· ·
SUMMARY AND KEY TAKEAWAYS
· ·

▸ Economic profits and economic profit growth are always highly concentrated—driven by differences in market economics and competitive position.

▸ Profit concentrations are often difficult to see, especially if management reports do not provide a breakdown of economic profitability by business and business segment. However, this disadvantage can be quickly overcome without a major overhaul of a company's reporting system.

▸ Management must understand where and why economic profit pools exist within their markets and businesses. Only then can managers think in a fact-based way about how to maximize the company's share of those profit pools and thereby maximize shareholder value.

▸ Managing for shareholder value is not just about eliminating unprofitable growth. It is also about freeing up resources and focusing innovation on capturing a greater share of economically profitable business segments.

▸ Companies that focus on capturing and maintaining a leading share of economic profits develop a reinvestment advantage that can lead to superior shareholder returns over an extended period of time.

CHAPTER 4
Focusing on the Highest Value-at-Stake Opportunities

. . . .

"One of the most important, if not the most important, roles of the chief executive is to establish and reinforce the right priorities."

—Jim Kilts, former Chairman and Chief Executive of Gillette, President and Chief Executive of Nabisco, and President of Kraft USA

. . . .

- Since economic profits are concentrated in every market and business, it follows that the opportunities to significantly improve shareholder value are also concentrated.

- The decisions made and actions taken on only a handful of issues and opportunities will likely determine whether your company outperforms or underperforms the competition.

- Knowing what those five to ten decisions and actions are, and focusing management time and talent on them, effectively turns good companies into great ones.

- Companies that consistently deliver superior shareholder returns manage to an explicit "value-improvement agenda." Managing that agenda requires an activist CEO.

All of the CEOs featured in this book have one thing in common. They constantly ask themselves, "What are the select few things that can *materially* improve my company's performance and shareholder value?"

These CEOs manage to an explicit shareholder-value-improvement agenda; they use this agenda to keep their organizations focused on the handful of things that will significantly increase their companies' share price.

When we talk about an agenda, we aren't using the word to mean what time topics are to be discussed at the next meeting. Instead, we are referring to a list of the most important issues and opportunities facing the company and a quantification of the potential dollar per share impact each issue or opportunity might have on the company's stock price. The CEOs featured in this book make certain that at least one member of their executive committee is personally responsible for seeing that each item on the corporate agenda is dealt with and resolved.

As issues are resolved, the list of value improvement opportunities is refreshed. This ensures that the top management team is always focused on driving the company to higher levels of performance.

This may seem like common sense, but as the old expression goes, "Common sense is anything but common."

See if this story sounds familiar: concerned that his company's share price is trading at a low multiple, the CEO of a Fortune 50 company summons his senior staff to a meeting. One member of the management team seizes the floor and says, in essence, not to worry, "I have identified over seventy different initiatives we can take to boost performance." And then he starts to read them off.

After item twenty-one, the CEO cuts him off. "Steve," he says, "the more initiatives you describe, the less confident I am that any one of them will achieve its objectives. We cannot possibly revive the patient with a hundred Band-Aids. We are going to have to identify a few major opportunities that will change our trajectory."

While all good management teams have a qualitative sense of the key issues and opportunities facing their businesses, the best executives are not satisfied with an intuitive sense of the relative importance of an issue. They quantify the economic profit and dollar per share impact those issues are likely to have for the company. They understand that without quantification, there is no way to prioritize. And without prioritization, the urgent overwhelms the material.

Agenda Management at Lloyds

Sir Brian Pitman at Lloyds was one of the most disciplined managers of shareholder value. He worked with his executive team every year to establish the corporate agenda. At least one member of his executive team would be responsible for seeing that each high-value-at-stake item was resolved. Pitman would usually assume personal responsibility for the highest value-at-stake opportunity.

This approach to managing the company served Pitman and his shareholders well. During his tenure as chief executive, Pitman doubled the market value of Lloyds (later Lloyds TSB) every three years for fifteen straight years.

Pitman's approach is not unique. In fact, most of the chief executives who have delivered superior shareholder returns over an extended period manage to an explicit value-improvement agenda. They do not allow the analyst community to dictate their company's agenda.

But how does an executive team go about defining and quantifying the highest value-at-stake issues facing their company? To illustrate, let's consider the case of MeadWestvaco.

Defining the Corporate Agenda at MeadWestvaco

By 2008, despite significant portfolio restructuring and repeated cost-reduction initiatives, MeadWestvaco (MWV) was still delivering below-average shareholder returns. It was then that Chairman and CEO John Luke decide to adopt a more disciplined approach to managing shareholder value.

He began with a company-wide assessment of where and why economic profits were being created and consumed across the corporation.

MWV's management and its board of directors had an intuitive sense of the relative performance of the company's business units and which ones were underperforming. But what they did not appreciate until the economic profit of each business was measured, was just how concentrated value creation was across the corporate portfolio and within each line of business, or why.

Luke picks up the story from there.

"First, we were surprised to learn that less than $4 billion of the total $7 billion of corporate revenue was generating positive economic profits and contributing to shareholder value. Why were we surprised? Well, over 90 percent of the company's revenues were generating positive operating profits; however, when the full cost of capital and shared service costs were allocated to these businesses, we realized that over half of its businesses were actually consuming shareholder value."

Luke goes on to say, "Management had been investing to grow all of the businesses that had positive operating profits. But with every dollar of top-line growth, the economically unprofitable businesses were destroying more and more shareholder value.

"Once we began to appreciate the size of the problem and the extent of the upside opportunity that this concentration represented, we started to investigate *why* each business unit was economically profitable or unprofitable and *what* could be done to improve the margins of the economically unprofitable businesses and more aggressively expand the economically profitable ones.

"Until we benchmarked the profitability of our competitors in each market, we didn't know how much of the company's underperformance was driven by bad market economics and how much was due to our competitive position in those markets," says Luke.

The bottom of Figure 4.1 shows what they found.

Luke goes on to describe how his management team used this information to establish the company's value-improvement agenda. "We used this improved understanding to group our businesses into three categories.

"Group One contained businesses that were participating in attractive markets where the average competitor was generating economic profits. These were also businesses in which we had a competitive advantage and higher economic profit margins than most competitors. These businesses warranted further investment and new growth opportunities needed to be developed.

"Group Two contained economically unprofitable businesses that could be turned around with a change in strategy.

"Finally, in Group Three were businesses that were participating in economically unattractive markets, markets where the sum of the economic profits of all competitors was negative. These businesses were also competitively disadvantaged relative to other market participants. In order for these businesses to generate economic profits we would need to find a way to become significantly advantaged or we would remain economically unprofitable. If we could not find a way to significantly improve our competitive position, we would need to withdraw resources from these businesses so they could be better employed elsewhere."

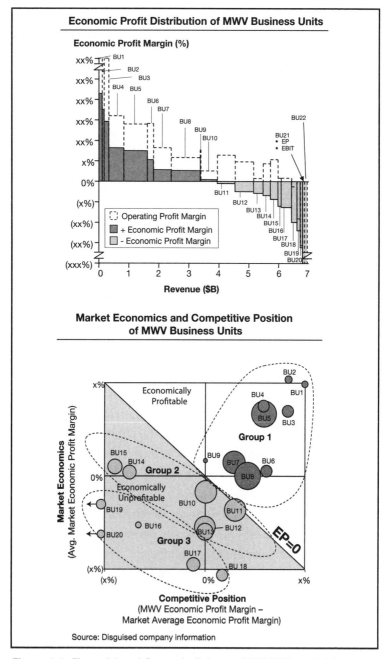

Figure 4.1: Financial and Strategic Drivers of MWV Shareholder Value, 2008

Armed with this financial and strategic assessment, the MWV leadership team was able to define and quantify a clear and concise corporate value-improvement agenda. (See Figure 4.2.)

Each member of MWV's executive committee assumed ownership of one or more of the agenda items and, over the course of the

	Group 1: Invest to grow		Group 2: Focus and optimize		Group 3: Restructure or withdraw investment	
Business Units	BU 1 through 10		BU 11 through 16		BU 17 through 20	
% of Total:	2008 (A)	2012 (F)	2008 (A)	2012 (F)	2008 (A)	2012 (F)
• Sales	55%	64%	30%	28%	15%	8%
• Capital Employed	50%	60%	29%	29%	21%	11%
• Economic Profit	147%	97%	(56%)	12%	(91%)	(9%)
Economic Profit Margin	5%	8%	(3%)	2%	(9%)	(5%)

Source: MeadWestvaco

Figure 4.2: Value Improvement at MeadWestvaco

next few months, they worked with line management to formulate and evaluate strategic alternatives for addressing each business on the agenda. The net result of this focus was agreement on specific strategy and resource allocation changes across the company. Over the next two years, there was a relentless focus on executing these changes.

"We had very specific plans and execution targets for each of the high value-at-stake items on the agenda," Luke says. "We worked as aggressively on investing to grow the profitable parts of our portfolio as we did on fixing or disinvesting from the value-consuming parts.

"One of the highest-value opportunities was expanding our packaging business in Brazil. The Brazilian market had good margins, was growing nicely, and our business in Brazil was economically profitable and competitively advantaged. We identified an opportunity to leverage our strong strategic position and made a commitment to invest the better part of $500 million in expanding our capacity in Brazil.

"By burdening the company with a $500-million investment, it was clear to everyone we were looking to the future. We were willing to realize economic profit losses in the short run against the promise of significantly improving our EP-generating trajectory going forward. The discounted value of that projected EP stream was clearly accretive to shareholder value. It has been a real lesson that we point to across the company to show that we're committed to growth and willing to invest, so long as it is attractive, value-creating growth. And it proves to everyone in the company that we are going to shift investment to opportunities that have the greatest potential for increasing economic profit growth.

"Situations like Brazil are the sorts of things that my team and I focus on and review regularly," Luke says. "They have become the core of our agenda with our board of directors. And we've built them into a process of very directed, very specific, quarterly conversations with each of the businesses."

This focus on resolving a specific list of high value-at-stake issues and opportunities proved far more effective in moving the company forward than any broad articulation of a corporate strategy. The net result was a dramatically improved business mix and competitive position. (See Figures 4.3 and 4.4.)

Between 2008 and 2010, MWV delivered significant improvements in overall economic profit growth. While the competition delivered a 31 percent return to shareholders over that time period, MWV delivered a 60 percent increase in shareholder value, double that of its peers.

The company has realized such significant benefits from adopting an agenda-based approach to managing shareholder value that the top management team now refreshes its list of the highest value-at-stake issues and opportunities each year.

Role of the Corporate Strategy Officer

Pleased with the initial results, MWV created a new position—chief strategy officer—to help institutionalize and maintain a more strategic approach to managing the company's shareholder value growth. While responsibility for developing strategy alternatives still resides with the business units, the chief strategy officer serves as a resource, helping both the business units and executive team refresh the company's agenda and evaluate strategic and resource allocation alternatives.

"I would strongly recommend that any company that adopts a value-based approach to managing their business establish a similar position. Our chief strategy officer is focused on helping teach and reinforce decision-making standards across our company and serves as a clearinghouse for strategic decision making and agenda setting for the company," says Luke. "It's less about having an enforcer than it is having someone who can work closely with the CEO and business unit leaders and be a resource for people across the enterprise who want to craft and successfully implement a winning strategy."

The typical reaction would be to have someone already in the C-suite, such as the CFO, take on these responsibilities. Luke understands, but disagrees.

"That was one of the alternatives we thought about," he says. "It is a lot to ask of someone who has been in the organization, who has been moving up the learning curve along with everyone else, to take on this burden.

"The CFO has plenty to do, and the chief strategy officer role is a full-time role. By having a full-time person, you really ensure that the focus is all about the company's strategic agenda and alternatives. That person analyzes, teaches, and helps shape corporate and business unit

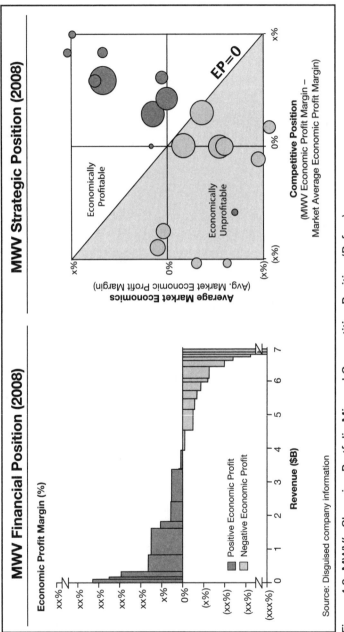

Figure 4.3: MWV's Changing Portfolio Mix and Competitive Position (Before)

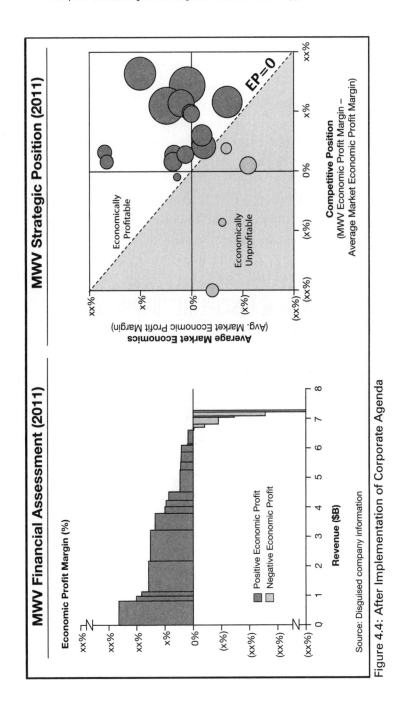

Figure 4.4: After Implementation of Corporate Agenda

strategies, which continue to improve the economic profit growth and shareholder value of the company.

"Our finance people and our strategy people work very closely together. So I don't view it as adding a layer. But for those who see it that way, it is a very inexpensive layer, relative to the substantial benefits that can come from the proper pursuit of the role."

Agenda management has become the primary means by which Luke steers the company. By adding new issues to the agenda as others are resolved, management remains continually focused on outperforming both its competition and investor expectations.

CASCADING THE DISCIPLINE THROUGHOUT THE ORGANIZATION

Agenda management should not be the sole domain of corporate management. Each business unit should also be continually updating its own value-improvement agenda, as John Luke goes on to explain. "We have established a process at MWV where each of the businesses identifies its own five or six high value-at-stake priorities, the big needle movers. Quarter in and quarter out, we are constantly asking our business unit managers to identify new strategic opportunities to improve economic profit growth. We want them to be thinking in a refreshed fashion about what's changed in the markets, what we have learned that might represent better opportunity going forward, and what newer and better things we can do to grow profitably."

In so doing, line management is encouraged to constantly focus on those things that will have a material impact on increasing the shareholder value contribution of each business unit and to stop doing those things that will not. That's no small point.

Certainly, every business is involved in some activities that are not helping the company make more money. The agenda-management process is an opportunity to question those activities. If you determine that some activities are not important, you simply stop doing them.

Taking the "No Regrets" Actions Quickly

"Without exception, the first set of value-at-stake issues you identify are almost always around dumb things you've been doing and never thought of as being dumb," says Travis Engen, former CEO of Alcan. "When you realize they are, you stop doing them.

"For example, our metals business had a hedging operation, because, well, historically the company had had one. The notion was that we were buying futures and selling futures in aluminum to protect ourselves against currency changes and price changes in aluminum.

"But when we looked back over time, we saw this operation was costing us $50 million a year and had basically zero benefit. We had been uniformly poor—both positively and negatively—in projecting what the price of aluminum was going to be. And we had, by the way, very detailed market knowledge of production and production assets. We were the best in the industry when it came to those things. But it had no relationship whatsoever to the price of aluminum that we could detect. We were always guessing wrong. So we eliminated $50 million worth of costs. You discover these sorts of things when you really start digging."

Developing Business Unit Agendas at Gillette

At the time Jim Kilts took over as chief executive of Gillette, Wall Street was clamoring for him to spend time either fixing or getting rid of the troubled Duracell battery division, which was acquired by a previous administration.

While Kilts knew that the Duracell issue needed to be addressed, it simply wasn't one of the highest value-at-stake issues facing the company. (See Figure 4.5.) Fixing Duracell would have only improved Gillette's stock price by a couple of dollars per share. A far more pressing issue was the declining share and profitability of the

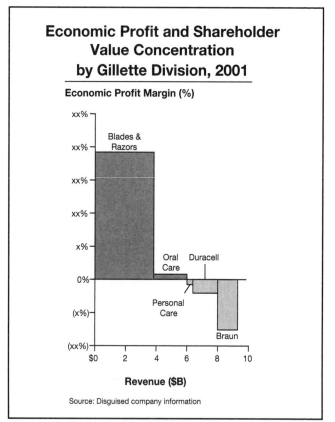

Figure 4.5: Economic Profit and Shareholder Value Concentration at Gillette, 2001

company's Blades and Razors (B&R). A slight improvement in the growth rate of the B&R business would increase Gillette's stock price by several dollars per share.

However, Gillette already had more than 85 percent of the economic profits in the B&R market worldwide—more than four times greater than Schick, BIC, and Wilkinson combined. While Kilts needed to improve the economic profit growth of the B&R business, he knew he could not do so by just asking the business to do what it had been doing, only better.

Kilts was convinced that attempts to drive performance through top-down targets, without reconsidering the business strategy, would cause the business to enter what he calls the "circle of doom"—setting unrealistic performance expectations without first addressing the business strategy. He knew this would only lead to short-term tactics to improve near-term results, for example, cutting "good" costs that were essential to differentiating the brand and discounting price to push short-term volume. (See Figure 4.6.)

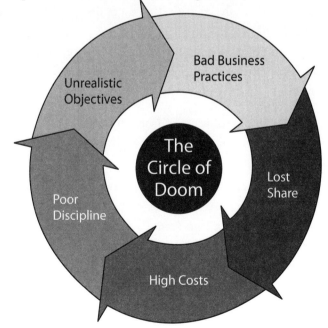

Figure 4.6: Jim Kilts's "Circle of Doom"[6]

Instead, Kilts asked the B&R business team to dig deeper to better understand where and why economic profits were being made across the global hair removal market and to identify what changes in business strategy had the greatest potential to improve economic profit growth of the entire market. Figure 4.7 lays out the resulting strategic agenda that led to the transformation of the B&R industry and Gillette's business.

Over the course of the next four years, Gillette launched a new line of premium disposable razors, including razors designed specifically for women. The company also began offering other high-margin hair removal products, like creams and waxes, that were favored by female consumers in Europe. And most importantly, the business changed its marketing strategy, shifting resources from advertising to new product trials. Kilts reasoned that consumers would be more likely to switch from older to new, higher-priced, better-performing products once they actually tried the product. So the company began mailing samples of its newest, most innovative blade and razor design to consumers across the country. The cost of the promotion program was quickly offset by the profit gains from new product sales.

As a result of these and other changes, Gillette's corporate-wide performance improved in every financial and customer market dimension:

- Net sales increased from $8.1 billion in 2001 to $11.4 billion in 2005, a 9 percent compounded annual growth rate (CAGR).

- Earnings before interest, taxes, depreciation, and amortization (EBITDA) increased from $2.2 billion to $3.7 billion over the same period, a 14 percent CAGR. Importantly, EBITDA increased meaningfully in each of Gillette's five global business units.

- Net working capital fell from 22 percent of net sales in 2000 to less than 1 percent in 2004.

Blades & Razors Business – Value-Improvement Agenda

Highest Value-at-Stake Issues & Opportunities	Business Model Change	EP Improvement ($)
• Conversion to higher-value products more responsive to consumer trial than advertising	• Dramatically shifted investment from advertising to sampling	+++
• Unsatisfied consumer need for high-end disposable products, especially in the female segment	• Launched first premium disposable and first female-specific "high-end" product (Venus)	++
• Lack of affordability compromising expansion in low GDP per capita markets	• Refocused commercial strategies on disposables in Latin America and select European markets	++
• Underexploited market for female hair removal in Europe	• Acquired wax/cream business and repositioned brand from "shaving" to "hair removal"	++
• Slow time to market for new product innovations	• Restructured new product development and commercialization process	+

Source: Disguised company information

Figure 4.7: Gillette's Blades and Razors Business: Value-Improvement Agenda

- Operating margins increased from 21 percent in 2001 to 26 percent in 2005, reflecting profitable top-line growth and better cost management, somewhat offset by higher marketing spending.

- Market shares increased in businesses representing 90 percent of 2005 sales compared to only 30 percent of sales in 2001.

- Economic profit grew from $700 million to over $1.6 billion.

- Finally, Gillette's stock price rose from its low of $25.62 in April 2001 to $45.00 per share in 2004 and $53.94 in January 2005 at the time of its announced sale to Procter & Gamble, creating $26 billion of incremental shareholder value.

BECOMING AN ACTIVIST CEO

The best CEOs often think about their companies as activist investors do. As you know, activist investors use their equity stake in a corporation to put pressure—often public pressure—on management to make changes that will increase total shareholder returns.

If the idea of being a "corporate raider" makes you uncomfortable, picture yourself running a large private equity firm. Their mantra: "Our objective is to find the most value improvement in the shortest period of time possible."

Most of the CEOs who have been successful in delivering and sustaining superior shareholder returns take exactly the same approach.

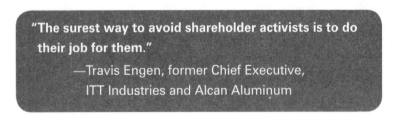

"The surest way to avoid shareholder activists is to do their job for them."

—Travis Engen, former Chief Executive, ITT Industries and Alcan Aluminum

This activist mindset should come as no surprise; indeed, it makes perfect sense, if you consider how shareholders view a company. They are looking for corporate management to outperform the competition and maximize the value of their shares, just as activist investors are trying to get a higher return on their investment than they could receive from putting their money elsewhere.

We have already talked about how economic profits are always highly concentrated within every company, no matter what. That means that it's quite possible that there is a manager three or four levels down the organizational chart from you who may have responsibility for a disproportionately large part of the company's economic profits.

Think back to the Gillette example. Kilts knew that the most significant opportunity to improve Gillette's shareholder value was to improve the growth of the blade and razor business.

Most CEOs would leave responsibility to the chain of command—the head of the division and their brand and regional management teams.

But an *activist* CEO takes a direct role in seeing that the traditional views about the business are challenged in order to arrive at the value maximizing strategy.

In the case of Gillette, the head of the B&R business and his team were extremely competent. However, they had strongly held views about the business that were limiting the strategic options that were being considered. With a bit of encouragement from Kilts and an updated set of financial and strategic facts, the management team was able to identify the business model improvements that significantly improved performance.

As CEO, your primary fiduciary responsibility is to the shareholders. You have the right to intrude whenever and wherever there is a significant amount of value at stake—even three or four levels down on the organizational chart. What should always be paramount is finding ways of increasing shareholder value, not respecting how the organization is structured.

Don Knauss at Clorox provides a variation on this: "There are occasions where I will say, 'Let's get out of this strict hierarchical mindset.' We may go down a level, or skip a couple, and say, 'This person needs to be on the strategy team, or that person needs to be on the operating team, or that person needs to be on the people-culture team, to make sure we get done what we want to get done.'"

You need the right people involved, no matter where they are in the official corporate structure, if you are to maximize shareholder value.

RELENTLESS FOCUS ON DOING WHAT MATTERS

The reason you need to focus on the value agenda is clear. But doing so within a large organization is difficult.

As Sir Brian Pitman explains, "It is a never-ending task to out-perform investor expectations, since those expectations are always increasing. To keep up requires a constant [focus on the] value-improvement agenda and agenda-management process."

Jim Kilts calls it staying focused on "doing what matters." As he describes, "It takes guts to say these are the things that really matter and I'll pay absolutely no attention to the rest. When you're young and impulsive, everything seems possible. Even doing everything at once doesn't seem daunting. But experience teaches you that nothing gets done when you try to do too much. You either whirl around in circles or slump into paralysis when facing endless options simultaneously."

While the relevance of this simple observation to the business world seems evident, it is baffling how many intelligent, well-trained, and experienced executives fail to heed it.

However, as MWV's John Luke says, "Organizations properly led will readily adopt this approach, because it is a way of ensuring you win. But like any other discipline or training regiment, despite all your good intentions, if you take your eye off the ball, the progress you're making can slowly be eroded.

"One of the many mistakes you can make is not having mechanisms in place that force the organization to remain focused on the highest value-at-stake issues and opportunities. Without them, you can find yourself once again responding to the day-to-day pressures in the marketplace. You can find yourself falling off the wagon."

"Establishing that discipline," says John Allison of BB&T, "is fairly straightforward: first, you get agreement on the most significant value-improvement opportunities. Then you establish responsibilities for developing strategies to capitalize on those opportunities. Then you put performance monitoring systems in place and align people's compensation, and then inspect what you expect. You inspect the heck out of it," he says with a laugh.

WHERE DO MANY COMPANIES GO WRONG?

Most companies do *not* have an explicit, quantified corporate value-improvement agenda. Instead, they may have a mission statement or corporate strategy they hope will guide behavior and the overall direction of the company. For example, one Fortune 500 company's mission statement is "to combine aggressive strategic marketing with quality products and services at competitive prices, to provide the best value for customers." While aspirational, such general statements of strategic intent pose four basic problems:

1. They are not specific enough to focus top management's attention and resources. While a corporation may be pursuing an overall corporate strategy, it is the *specific* issues and opportunities that need to occupy top management's time and attention. In other words, progress against a corporate strategy needs to be measured by the specific actions taken and the results achieved.

2. *They do not provide a consistent basis for prioritization.* In the absence of any other prioritization mechanism, management time is allocated to the most immediate demands, not the most important. It is amazing how near-term concerns crowd out the time that should be devoted to the strategic and resource allocation decisions that will truly impact performance.

3. *They are neither tangible enough, nor sufficiently quantified, to measure progress or drive accountability.* Agendas make explicit what is going to be managed and how progress will be measured, and as a result, what people should pay the most attention to. That's a key reason why agendas are commonplace in managing corporate restructurings and merger integrations. They provide clarity into objectives, a sense of urgency, and an absolute need to prioritize actions and resources.

4. *They do not provide the basis for making trade-off decisions.* Corporate mission statements and the like provide little direction for how to deal with the trade-offs inherent in most business decisions. If the mission is "to combine aggressive strategic marketing with quality products and services at competitive prices, to provide the best value for customers," how much "product quality" should be provided in exchange for the "competitive price"? And how much cost should be incurred to provide it? Managers are often left wondering not only which combination of quality, price, and cost is best, but also what actions they must take to deliver it. Being clear about the corporate agenda and the criteria by which trade-off decisions should be made allows management to define what the business will not do or will stop doing. Unless it is evident what a business must stop doing, it is impossible to focus on what must be done.

SUMMARY AND KEY TAKEAWAYS

▸ Only a handful of strategic decisions and actions will determine whether a business outperforms or underperforms the competition.

▸ Knowing what those five to ten things are, and focusing management time and talent on them, is what turns good companies into great ones.

▸ Defining and managing to an explicit value-improvement agenda is the primary means by which value-oriented CEOs guide their companies. In doing so, they are acting just as an activist investor would.

▸ Cascading this corporate value-improvement agenda into the business units ensures that all managers are focused on how they will contribute to the company's shareholder-value growth

▸ Managing to an explicit value-improvement agenda, and refreshing that agenda periodically, requires discipline and dedication on the part of the CEO to think and act like an activist investor.

CHAPTER 5
Differentiated Strategies and Differential Allocation of Resources

· ·

"If you want to be better than your competition, you can't do what they're doing. You've got to be different. Being different requires making different choices about where and how you compete."

— Travis Engen, former Chief Executive,
ITT Industries and Alcan Aluminum

· ·

- Good companies do things better; superior companies do things differently.

- Material gains in both economic profit growth and shareholder value come from fundamental improvements in the choices about *where* and *how* to compete.

- Strategic and resource allocation decisions must be based on facts, not just intuition. A factual understanding of the current and future drivers of market economics and competitive position is essential to making good decisions and provides the platform for developing truly innovative strategies.

- Competitive advantage, not diversification, reduces risk and maximizes economic profit growth and shareholder value.

Strategies need to be more than qualitative statements of intent, they must be specific descriptions of how a business intends to outperform the competition in creating greater:

1. *Customer value*, by better satisfying customer needs.
2. *Shareholder value*, by capturing a disproportionate share of economic profits.

The CEOs featured in this book have emphasized that strategies must define how a business will differentiate itself from the competition in order to capture a leading share of the economic profits. However, far too many business strategies do nothing more than describe the steps that will be taken to incrementally improve performance, in effect describing how a business will continue to do what is has been doing, only better.

What's wrong with that? Well, at one level, nothing. Continuous improvement is a good thing.

You may remember the following nursery rhyme:

Good, better, best.
Never let it rest
Until your good is better
And your better is best.

That advice still holds true. But since you have to assume the competition is going to be doing that as well, you need to ask yourself a higher-order question, namely, "Is the business strategy we're trying to optimize actually the best business strategy?"

Most companies don't ask that question. Without really being aware of it, they are assuming they are already marketing and selling the right products, at the right price, to the right customers, through the right channels, with the right supply-chain configuration.

But what if they aren't? Then they are spending all their time trying to optimize a sub-optimal business strategy.

In Chapter 2 we highlighted just how important competitive position is to a company's economic profitability and relative shareholder value growth. It is important to recognize that differences in competitive position are seldom driven by differences in operating efficiency; they are primarily driven by different choices companies make about where and how to compete.

> "Differences in competitive position are rarely due to doing the same thing better; they are usually due to doing things differently."
> —Don Knauss, Chairman and CEO, the Clorox Company

We hear managers say, "The competition is more efficient; they have higher margins than we do. We've got to benchmark their manufacturing process and their raw materials sourcing and their labor costs to find out how to replicate best demonstrated operating practices." But when they look at the data, they discover there is only a 5 percent difference in operating efficiency relative to the competitor. This doesn't explain why the competitor has 20 percent higher margins.

Upon further investigation, they usually find that the competitor has a different business mix and a greater share of the more profitable segments of the market.

The competitor is performing better because they have consciously made different choices about where and how to compete. They have focused their product development and commercial strategies on better satisfying the needs of the more profitable customers and, as a result, they are generating greater cash flow, which they then reinvest to further improve their differentiation.

> **"Doubling the share price every three years can't be accomplished by incremental changes; it requires major change and scrapping the old ways of doing things."**
>
> —Sir Brian Pitman, former Chairman and CEO, Lloyds TSB

So before you start trying to optimize performance, ask yourself whether you are pursuing the right business strategy. Some management teams get resentful when you ask that question; they say, "This is what we have been doing for the past fifteen years. Do you think we are stupid? Do you think we would pursue something that doesn't work?"

Our answer is no, but just because the business strategy has "worked" in the past doesn't mean it will "maximize" economic profit growth going forward. In all likelihood, market economics and the competitive landscape have changed since you last considered other strategic alternatives.

Don't Exit a Market, Change Your Focus

There are always economically unprofitable businesses in a corporate portfolio. A natural reaction, when you discover that a business has been consuming shareholder value, is to exit the business. We caution against this knee-jerk reaction.

Most businesses that are generating economic losses are not participating in chronically unprofitable markets, nor are they forever destined to be competitively disadvantaged. They have just been pursuing a bad strategy. In fact, management has probably been investing in economically unprofitable growth without even realizing it. However, there are certain to be economically profitable segments in the markets this business is serving or could be serving. Refocusing the businesses on the profitable segments of the market can have a remarkably positive impact on performance. Let's revisit the banking industry to illustrate this important point.

Refocusing on Profitable Segments: The U.S. Banking Industry

By the late 2000s the banking industry's troubles were sorely apparent. Years of poor lending practices led to unprecedented credit losses in mortgages, home-equity lending, and especially commercial real estate lending. Worse, retail banking, long a mainstay of bank profitability, was under pressure. Because of low interest rates and a flat yield curve, banks were earning lower spreads on deposits. New regulations limited the fees that banks could charge for bounced checks and for debit card transactions.

In addition to this collapse of the traditional revenue model, banks were also dealing with higher costs from years of expanding their branch networks—branches that customers were using less and less as they turned increasingly to online channels.

So how and where are banks able to grow profitably in this difficult environment? The answer lies in customer mix. After years of pursuing new checking-account customers (in the often vain hope of cross-selling these customers a mortgage or home-equity loan), a few banks began to recognize that the economic profits available in consumer banking—and more importantly, the economic profit growth—were very concentrated. So-called affluent and mass affluent customers (customers with at least $100,000 of investable assets) made up just 20 percent to 30 percent of the population but represented more than 80 percent of the total economic profit and all of the future economic profit growth potential in the consumer banking market.

Now, you may be thinking this is yet another version of the old saw about why people rob banks—because that's where the money is—and that banks should simply obtain more wealthy clients. While acquiring new wealthy clients would certainly be nice, prying these customers away from competitors with whom they already had relationships with these customers would not be easy or inexpensive. However, a handful of banks realized they already had relationships with many of these affluent customers.

When these banks profiled their retail customers, they found that as many as 40 percent of them were affluent or mass-affluent. But these clients' total assets had gone unrecognized for years and, as a result, the bank was underserving their own clients' wealth management needs. Many of these clients used their bank only for a secondary checking account or maybe some CDs. But few of them were being offered packages of comprehensive services—financial planning, investment advice, investment products, and the like. On the rare occasions when these customers were being fully served, they generated four to five times more economic profit and had a better mix of products, higher fee revenues, and better retention. But only 5 percent to 10 percent of these customers were currently being fully served by most banks.

Why? The reasons trace back to the bank's organization, processes, and information systems. While sophisticated tools exist to estimate clients' affluence based on their behavior and on publicly available data, many banks look only at the customer's products and balances within the bank. Thus they get caught in the self-fulfilling false-hood that only customers who have high balances with the bank are actually wealthy. As a result, they don't know which customers in their retail franchise are actually afflu-ent and which are not.

Even if they knew which customers were wealthy enough to target, most banks would have trouble acting on the information due to organizational barriers. Typi-cally, those responsible for managing wealthy customers are in a separate business unit from the retail business. The wealth management and retail businesses are often housed in different locations, have different incentives, and sometimes offer competing products and services. Some banks do try to encourage referrals across these organizational silos, usually through compensation incen-tives. But rarely is there a shared list of target clients, or a consistent marketing program and value proposition tailored specifically to expand the bank's relationships with these clients. Without that, banks find it very difficult to systematically bring the expertise and products of the wealth-management organization to affluent customers in the retail channel.

The result? Most banks fail to capture the full "share of wallet" of their own best customers, instead ceding the most profitable parts of these relationships to other finan-cial institutions.

The few banks that have succeeded in identifying the wealthy customers in their retail networks and have bro-ken down the barriers between organizational silos have significantly improved their economic profit growth. They have figured out how to capitalize on the customer's exist-ing relationship with the bank by investing in a consistent process for targeting and developing these relationships. These top performing banks benefit from a continuously improving customer mix that provides strong top- and bottom-line growth in an industry where both are shrink-ing. One bank that made this leap saw its average eco-nomic profit per client increase from $400 to $1,500 and significantly increased the contribution its retail banking and wealth management franchises were making to the bank's overall economic profit.

Not bad for a no-growth environment.

ASKING THE RIGHT QUESTIONS

There are three related questions every management team must be able to answer in order to define its optimal business strategy:

1. *Market economics.* What is the size and concentration of economic profits in the market and market segments where we compete—or would like to compete—now and in the future? Unless managers understand where and why economic profits are concentrated within a market, it will be impossible for them to know where and how to capture a greater share of those profits.

2. *Competitive position.* Who is best satisfying profitable customer needs and capturing a greater share of economic profits and how?

3. *Strategic alternatives.* What strategic alternatives are available that will maximize our sustainable share of available economic profits? Alternatives include changes in:

    a. *Participation:* Altering the mix of markets and market segments in which they participate.

    b. *Offer:* Improving the real or perceived differentiation

of their products and services, either by changing the characteristics of the offer or how those characteristics are marketed and promoted.

c. **Pricing:** Changing the price of individual products or the realized price of combined products and services.

d. **Operating configuration:** Changing how the offer is sourced, produced, distributed, sold, and serviced.

The top of Figure 5.1 lays these choices out graphically.

Decisions about these four dimensions of strategy, and how resources are allocated to implement them, will determine whether a business will outperform or underperform its competition. The importance of making strategic choices that create profitable differences between your business and your competitor's business cannot be overemphasized. Managers need to recognize that innovative strategic choices that lead to competitive advantage are as valuable as new product innovations in improving profitable growth.

> "Significant improvement in profitable growth and shareholder returns requires equally significant changes in the choices a company makes about where and how to compete."
> —John Luke, Chairman and CEO, MeadWestvaco

How do you know if the strategy you are pursuing is advantaged? It boils down to this: *if the business is gaining share of economic profits in a market, then it is pursuing an advantaged strategy. If it is losing share of economic profits, it isn't.* (See the bottom of Figure 5.1.)

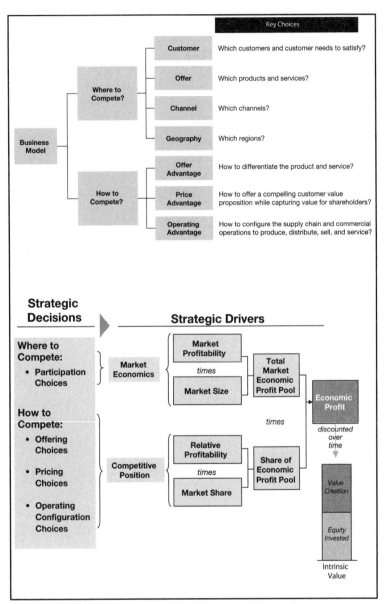

Figure 5.1: Strategic Alternatives: *Where* and *How* to Compete;
Strategic Decisions Affect Level of Economic Profits

TRANSLATING STRATEGIES INTO RESULTS

In order for a corporation to maximize shareholder value, each business unit must develop and execute the strategy that maximizes its contribution to corporate shareholder value.

CEOs should expect every business unit manager to know:

1. Where and why economic profits are concentrated in the markets they serve or plan to serve, now and in the future.

2. What participation, offer, pricing, and operating configuration choices will maximize their business's share of available economic profits in each served market.

3. What actions and resources will be required to implement those strategic choices and what operating and financial performance can be expected from those actions.

For this to occur, the corporation needs a consistent set of standards and processes for making strategic and resource allocation decisions.

The specific standards and processes used by most value-managed companies will be discussed in Chapter 6. But for now, it is easy to see why decision standards and processes are important. After all, how often have you sat through annual strategy sessions as one business unit head after another discusses the threats and opportunities they are facing in conceptual terms, followed with a single proposed strategy to pursue?

How will you know whether the strategy being proposed is the best one—the one that will maximize economic profit growth—if you have not been provided with a factual description of the sources and drivers of economic profit and if only one viable strategic alternative is being proposed?

Henry Kissinger tells a wonderful story about how the Pentagon used to do just that in presenting "options." As Kissinger describes it, they always offered the President three choices:

1. Do nothing and be overrun by the Soviets.
2. Do something that will assure mutual nuclear destruction.
3. Do what the Pentagon wanted the administration to approve.

If the CEO and top management are to have confidence that shareholders' capital is being allocated only to those strategies that will maximize shareholder value—and being redirected away from those that are consuming value—they need to participate in a more substantial dialogue with the company's business units. To do this efficiently, the better CEOs have set up a systematic process for discussing and approving business unit strategies. The process involves three formal sessions with each business unit team:

1. *Fact-base discussions.* The first session focuses on understanding the current and future economics of the markets in which the business unit participates, its relative competitive position in each of those markets, and the resulting concentrations of economic profit potential across each business segment. The purpose of these initial discussions is to reach a shared understanding of the fact base and the highest value-at-stake issues and opportunities facing the business.

2. *Strategic alternatives discussions.* The second session focuses on the strategic alternatives available to the business and the economic profit growth that each alternative is forecast to produce. The outcome of this discussion is an agreement on where and how the business will compete.

3. *Implementation plans and commitments discussions.* The third and final session focuses on the action plans, performance commitments, and resources required to implement

the strategy. The outcome of this session is an agreement to the business unit's performance targets and milestones. These plans serve as the basis for establishing the business unit budgets and resource allocation. In addition, the detailed implementation plans are also used to coordinate actions between the business unit and various functions that provide it with support.

Figure 5.2 illustrates this three-step communication and decision process.

Now let's look at a few examples of how this process works in practice.

Transforming Alcan

"When I first became chief executive at Alcan," says Travis Engen, "I worked with my executive leadership team to establish our corporate shareholder performance and economic profit growth goal. At that time, the average cost of capital in the minerals and mining industry was around 10 percent. That was the level of total shareholder returns Alcan would likely deliver if we matched investor expectations for cash flow and economic profit growth going forward. At that rate of return, Alcan would double shareholder value in about seven or eight years.

"However, the companies that historically delivered shareholder returns in the top quartile of their peer group doubled shareholder value in about five years. In other words, they delivered compounded annual shareholder returns of 15 percent or more. So we adopted the corporate goal of doubling Alcan's shareholder value in five years.

"It was initially difficult to get our business managers to consider strategy alternatives. I understood that. They were all good managers and were already doing what they thought was best for the business. But they had not previously been managing the business for maximum economic profit growth. They did not have the level of in-depth

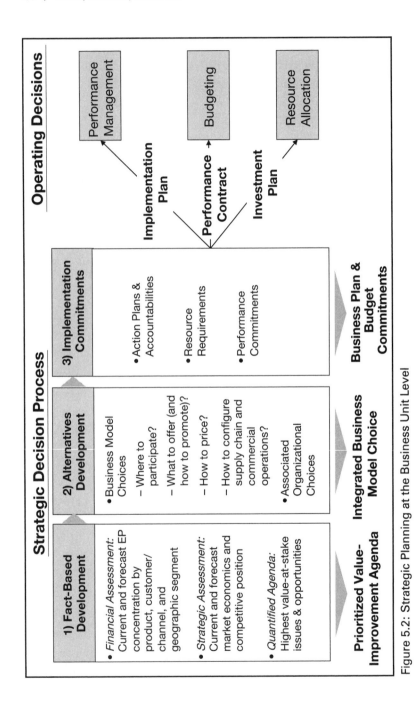

Figure 5.2: Strategic Planning at the Business Unit Level

understanding of where economic profits were concentrated in each of their markets, and they did not understand their customer and competitor economics as well as they would eventually.

"So we helped the business unit teams understand that if the corporation was going to double shareholder value in five years, then on average, each business unit would have to double its own contribution to shareholder value in five years. It quickly became clear that the historical approach these businesses had taken to their markets would not deliver that level of economic profit growth.

"Linking these stretch targets to the company's overall shareholder value performance goals served as a very useful way of getting each business to consider strategic alternatives. Of course, we did not unilaterally demand that these 'provisional' targets become the final budget goals for each business. Only after we thoroughly considered the range of realistic strategic alternatives available to each business did we agree to their budget targets." (See Figure 5.3.)

"However, it took the introduction of 'provisional' targets to get the businesses to seriously start analyzing the concentration of economic profits in each of their respective markets. When they did, they began to really understand what was driving the economic profit growth and the reason competitors were earning more or less than they were in each market."

Engen goes on to describe the strategic decision standards and process he used at Alcan. "We had three in-depth discussions with each management team. In the first review, we discussed what was driving market economics and competitive position and the big opportunities facing each business. From that discussion, we reached agreement on the highest value-at-stake issues and opportunities.

"In the second meeting, we discussed the strategic and operating alternatives available to the business. Sometimes they were apparent, sometimes there were surprises, and sometimes a member of the executive committee had to suggest an alternative that the business had not considered or was unwilling to consider.

"The forecasted economic profit for each strategic alternative was also presented. Since we now had a very in-depth, fact-based understanding of market and competitor economics, we had better confidence in those forecasts. You could clearly see when a business was putting forth unrealistic 'hockey stick' forecasts. After a while, there was real integrity to the forecasting and decision-making process. The weight of opinion was now based on facts, not personality, and the decisions became much more aligned with the interests of the shareholders. Of course, it would have been difficult for a business-unit team to recommend any strategic alternative other than the one that was forecasted to deliver the greatest economic profit growth.

"The third meeting was focused entirely on what needed to be done to implement the strategy—what actions would be taken, by what group of people, when, who was accountable for ensuring that action, what were the interim operating and financial results we expected from those actions, and what resources would be required, and when, to realize those results.

"This process significantly improved not just the understanding of the business but also the commitment to the strategy by both the business unit teams and the executive team. It also fundamentally changed the budget and resource allocation process. No longer were strategies something that were separate from the budgets, and no longer were we approving projects with forecasted internal rates of return of 25 percent year after year, only to find that the business continued to deliver 8-percent returns. The strategic decisions, resource allocation process, and budgeting process were now aligned and consistent.

"This decision process was not a one-time thing," Engen concludes. "It became the way we managed the business on an ongoing basis. We monitored performance of our strategy on a quarterly basis

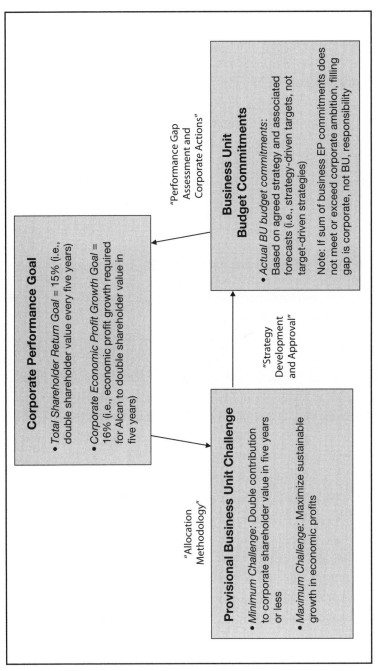

Figure 5.3: Performance Goals and Total Shareholder Return Ambitions

and addressed strategic issues and alternatives as they came up, not at the end of the year as part of some synthetic annual strategy exercise.

"This also became the foundation for how I interacted with my board of directors. Our business unit managers periodically presented to the board, informing our directors of any material changes in market economics or our competitive position, as well as the strategic alternatives that were being considered and why we were pursuing the strategies we were pursuing. As a result of this level of disciplined communication, the board was not only well-informed, but we were able to get far greater leverage from our directors."

Abbott Laboratories Diagnostic Division Turnaround

Abbott Labs provides an example of how the same three-phase decision process helps both corporate and business unit management address challenging situations and agree to material changes in business strategy.

The Diagnostics Division was one that Chairman and CEO Miles White knew quite well; he began his career at Abbott there. However, over the decade since he had left the division to become CEO, the diagnostic industry had changed dramatically. The cost of the testing equipment that manufacturers leased to diagnostic testing labs had increased almost tenfold, and the margins earned on the assay sales and other products and services that were associated with each machine placement had decreased significantly.

Management realized that margins were declining, but they did not appreciate that profitability had decreased to the point where the Diagnostics Division was actually destroying shareholder value. As sales continued to grow in almost every geographic region, more and more economic losses were realized and more shareholder value was being consumed.

White considered selling the division to General Electric in

2007 but decided to try to turn the business around instead. So he instructed the division's management to take a more granular, shareholder-value-based view of the business.

As you can see in Figure 5.4, this assessment highlighted how the division management was being misled, by looking only at the operating profits of the division. A detailed review of the business revealed just how concentrated the economic profits were by customer segment within each geographic region.

"A deeper understanding of customer needs and economics," says White, "caused us to consider a whole range of strategic alternatives that had not previously been considered. These new facts helped challenge the long-standing conventional views about what was driving industry profitability and our competitive position.

"The business had to make some tough choices in order to focus on those segments of the market in which we had a competitive advantage," White says. "It was not easy. There is a huge commercial lab, probably one of our two largest customers in the U.S., that always wants a long-term contract, which meant every time our contract was up we are bidding against our competitors to extend the agreement. Well, it turns out that the price we were giving them was already lower than what was economically profitable. Once we understood that we could not be economically profitable at the price needed to extend the contract, we walked away from millions of dollars worth of revenue—business we already had—because we would not bid lower than our economic cost. We lost the business and improved our economic profits because we got rid of a piece of business that was losing money."

The money that would have been lost by extending economically unprofitable contracts was reinvested in new product innovations and profitable customer relationships. As a result of this discipline and refocusing of the business, the Diagnostics Division has continued to achieve top-line growth—growth that is now contributing to Abbott's stock price.

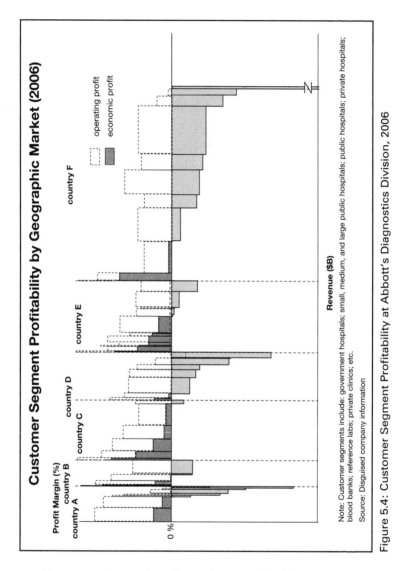

Figure 5.4: Customer Segment Profitability at Abbott's Diagnostics Division, 2006

Figure 5.5 shows what changed as a result of the analysis, while Figure 5.6 shows the improvement in ADD performance that was realized.

Abbott Diagnostics' Business Model Choices

	Prior Choices	New Choices
Market Participation	• Serve all customers, especially large volume accounts, to develop scale	• Focus on profitable market segments where Abbott has a competitive advantage
Price Position	• Discount price to gain share	• Price to capture share of profits
Offering Position	• Invest in product breadth to gain industry-wide market share	• Invest in differentiation to drive share in profitable segments
Operating Position	• Distribute sales force across all markets to maximize volume and manufacturing utilization	• Focus sales force on profitable market segments and rationalize excess capacity

Source: Disguised company information

Figure 5.5: Abbott Diagnostics Division (ADD) Business Model Choices

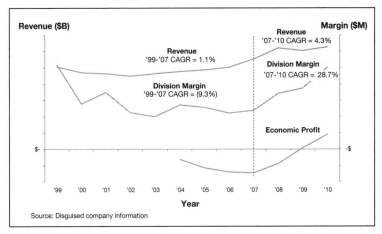

Source: Disguised company information

Figure 5.6: Abbott Diagnostics Division (ADD) Business Performance

DIFFERENTIATION VS. DIVERSIFICATION

Some executives resist the notion of strategic focus. A past Merrill Lynch chief executive epitomized that resistance when he passionately stated, "We need to participate in all markets, whether they are economically profitable and we are competitively advantaged or not, in order to reduce our risk and maximize our opportunity." The consequences of that point of view are evidenced in the shareholder returns, and ultimately in the fate, of Merrill Lynch and any number of companies that have pursued diversification and top-line growth without regard for its contribution to shareholder value.

Companies that are best at delivering shareholder value growth recognize that competitive advantage, not diversification, minimizes risk and maximizes opportunity. Warren Buffett has been advocating just that philosophy for years. When you hear Buffett speak about his investment strategy, he will say, "Risk diversification and risk minimization does not come from putting my chips all over the board. It comes from focusing my chips in the places where I have a decisive competitive advantage." What Buffett is talking about is pursuing a focused and advantaged investment strategy. Not only is this how Buffett (whose net worth of $39 billion in 2011 made him the second richest man in America) invests but it is how the companies in the Berkshire Hathaway portfolio think about strategy.

Sir Brian Pitman echoed Buffett's perspective in his May 2003 presentation at the CEO Summit in St. Paul-de-Vence, France, when he said, "It used to be thought that diversifying your risk reduces your risk. But not if it ends up in weak market positions and low, or negative, cash flow. The real risk is that you enter markets in which you don't have a competitive advantage. Chasing market share frequently ends in tears. Profitability and competitive advantage result in high growth and market share—not the other way around. Companies with high multiples have chosen focus over diversity. Outsource diversification to shareholders."

It seems that Mark Twain's Pudd'nhead Wilson got it right when he said, "Behold, the fool saith, 'Put not all thine eggs in the one basket' but the wise man saith, 'Put all your eggs in the one basket and—WATCH THAT BASKET!'"

In addition to pursuing differentiated strategies, companies must also differentially allocate resources. However, in many companies, investment dollars tend to be allocated in proportion to the existing capital base of each business. That may seem "fair," but economically it makes little sense. Resources should be differentially allocated to the businesses that will create the most value, which are not necessarily the ones with the largest existing capital base.

New capital requests from businesses producing negative economic profits should always be viewed with skepticism. Such requests are always accompanied by attractive internal rate-of-return calculations and explanations of why this latest round of investments will "turn around" the business. However, unless there is clear evidence that the business is going to pursue a different, more economically profitable strategy than it has in the past, these requests should be denied.

Yes, of course, there will always be new products or businesses that for a time generate negative profits while in investment mode, but management needs to ensure that it does not fund chronically unprofitable investments.

The point here is simple: you must link capital-investment decisions to strategic decisions and actively seek to withdraw both capital and human resources from businesses and market segments that cannot be made to create value, reallocating those resources to ones that can.

"Sustainable improvement in economic profit growth requires a continual reallocation of resources away from business strategies that do not create value and toward those that do."

—John Luke, Chairman and CEO, MeadWestvaco

We end this particular discussion by repeating a key point made earlier: capturing a disproportionate share of market profits creates a sustainable reinvestment advantage. And this reinvestment advantage creates enduring competitive advantage. Don't squander this advantage by allocating resources to value-consuming parts of your business portfolio.

MAINTAINING THE DISCIPLINE

Making the kinds of changes we have just talked about can be a hard sell, as Jim Kilts is the first to admit. "That's why you need the data to demonstrate what you need to do to win."

John Allison of BB&T agrees: "You discipline everyone with logical reasoning and the facts and the numbers."

This requires a major commitment on the part of the C-suite, but as John Luke points out, that is nothing new.

"Any kind of change in an organization requires determined leadership engagement. Establishing a disciplined set of decision standards and processes requires a lot of education and follow-through," he says. "The hard part is ensuring that you sustain that approach to managing the company. This requires continuous communication and reinforcement."

Miles White concurs, "One of the things that we made sure we did at Abbott was educate across boundaries. We introduced this methodology in various parts of the world and across various parts of the business. When we were done explaining it, people understood why and understood that this was all about creating a baseline for a winning strategy going forward.

"As a result, I think we're better at targeting market segments and customers. And I think we're better at understanding real returns as opposed to just P&L profit. I think there's a better appreciation for returns in general and for economic profit in particular. And I believe there is a better appreciation of investment in general and what is an attractive market to go into and what isn't. We are asking more of the right questions that filter out poor economic decisions."

As Lloyds' Sir Brian Pitman points out, managing for value is different from the way most companies are run. However, as he saw first-hand—and we have observed in working with some of the world's best companies—there is no doubt that it works. But—and it is a huge but—Pitman repeatedly said:

- "Generating consistently superior shareholder returns is the most challenging task a company can set for itself."
- "It is a tough discipline to accept."
- "People will wiggle like mad to escape that discipline."
- "It requires extraordinary commitment and belief to stick to it over the long haul."

WHERE DO MANY COMPANIES GO WRONG?

Given the influence that strategy has on corporate and business performance, and the amount of time and resources that are devoted to strategy development, it is discouraging to observe how few companies are able to translate their strategies into superior performance.

One of the primary reasons is that "superior performance" is not well defined at the beginning of the strategy development process. Too many strategies suffer from the old adage "If you can't define where you want to go, any road will get you there."

Even if the end objective is clear, many corporate and business unit strategies fail to address the major trade-off decisions facing the business. For example, what segments of the market will the business serve and not serve and how will the trade-off between growth and margins be managed.

Finally, most strategies completely fail to define how the business will differentiate itself from the competition. Instead of defining what the business will do differently, it is more likely to define how the business will match industry best practices.

Even with the shortcomings listed above, most business strategies are accompanied by forecasts of above industry growth, margins and return on capital. It should come as no surprise that such strategies fail to deliver their promised results.

For strategies to be successful, they must be based upon:

- a clear definition of winning,
- a factual understanding of the economics of the markets in which the business chooses to compete and its relative competitive position in those markets,
- specific choices about where and how to compete that economically differentiate the business from its competition,

and they must be translated into specific action plans, performance commitments and resource requirements, that are used to drive budget and resource allocation decisions.

SUMMARY AND KEY TAKEAWAYS

▸ In order for a corporation to maximize shareholder value, each business in the corporate portfolio must develop and execute the strategy that maximizes its contribution to corporate shareholder value.

▸ Whether consciously or unconsciously, all businesses have made choices about where and how to compete. These choices ultimately determine whether the business gains or loses share of the economic profit in the market in which it competes.

▸ To gain share of economic profits, a business must be economically differentiated. The strategy must define how the business will do a better job than its competition in creating customer value and capturing a portion of that value for the company's shareholders in the form of economic profits.

▸ Differentiated strategies require explicit choices. To make these choices well, management must have a factual understanding of what is driving market economics, competitive position, and economic profit concentration.

▸ If strategies are to realize their promised results, they must be translated into implementation plans, performance commitments, and resource requirements. Only then can strategies drive budgeting and resource allocation decisions.

CHAPTER 6
Building an Advantaged Organization and an Ownership Culture

"I used to think that better management was a means to creating shareholder value. I now believe that shareholder value is a means to creating better management."

— Sir Brian Pitman, former Chairman and CEO, Lloyds TSB

- The culture of an organization is the result of the beliefs and organizational conditions that have been established.

- Most companies have not designed their organizations with the express intent of maximizing shareholder value growth. As a result, major organizational impediments stand in the way of realizing that outcome.

- Companies that have established the right beliefs and organizational conditions have built a culture where employees think and act like entrepreneurial owners. That culture is the ultimate source of sustainable competitive advantage and superior shareholder returns.

As the CEO, you and your executive team face two key challenges in delivering and sustaining superior shareholder value growth.

First, you need to ensure the strategies and resources are in place to maximize the economic profit growth of each business unit and the entire corporation.

Second, you must establish the organizational beliefs and conditions that increase the odds that the daily decisions and actions of the hundreds, if not thousands, of employees across your company are aligned with shareholder interests. You need to instill this behavior because, after all, you and your executive team cannot possibly be personally involved in every decision that influences corporate performance.

There are six organizational conditions that individually and collectively have a significant influence on employee behavior:

1. **Governing Objective** of the company
2. **Roles and Responsibilities** of executive team and line managers
3. **Business Boundaries and Reporting Relationships**
4. **Decision Standards and Processes**
5. **Incentive Practices**
6. **Education and Capabilities Development**

When companies get these conditions right, they are able to establish a culture where employees are more likely to think and act like entrepreneurial owners. These companies develop a true organizational advantage over their competition.

"An ownership culture is the ultimate source of sustainable competitive advantage."

—John Allison, former Chairman and Chief Executive, BB&T

There is a direct connection between the beliefs and organizational conditions that exist in a company and the strategies that those companies adopt and implement, and therefore, the financial performance and shareholder value they generate. Figure 6.1 underscores the point.

At most companies, the roles and responsibilities, business boundaries, decision processes, and incentive practices have not been designed with the objective of managing shareholder value. More often than not, they are a consequence of the company's heritage, an outgrowth of past political compromises, acquisitions, or leadership transitions.

As a result, even if managers are interested in improving economic profit growth, they face any number of organizational impediments, roadblocks that stand in the way of making the proper choices and taking the right actions.

Getting your managers to focus on and actually achieve economic profit growth takes more than just introducing a new measure of profitability and linking it to compensation. It requires consistent alignment of all organizational conditions that impact management behavior.

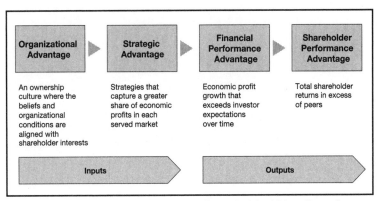

Figure 6.1: Achieving and Sustaining Shareholder Value Growth

Given the importance of this topic, this chapter will discuss each of the six organizational conditions listed above separately. Each section will provide examples of how successful chief executives have implemented a series of organizational changes that have enabled their company to sustain superior performance over an extended time period.

Don't Try This at Work

For a quick explanation of why simply focusing on or measuring economic profits is not enough if you want to maximize shareholder returns—and why you must also address governance processes, decision standards, incentive practices, and management capabilities—look no further than this short excerpt from the *Harvard Business Review*.

In a sidebar to their article, "Managing for Value: It's Not Just About the Numbers," INSEAD professors Philippe Haspeslagh, Tomo Noda, and Fares Boulos correctly point out what can go wrong at companies trying to manage for shareholder value—what they call "value-based management (VBM)."

How *Not* to Do VBM[7]

A well-known global company participating in our survey is an excellent study in how not to implement VBM. Although it proclaimed that value creation was its raison d'être, the company did little beyond adopting an economic profit metric as a performance measure.

For a start, the link between employee bonuses and shareholder value was tenuous. Although a proportion of the bonus was tied to the share price performance of the company and to the economic profit targets of its businesses, several other factors also played a part in determining its size. As a result, employees could game the system by focusing on whatever measures they favored. Training was also skimpy: less than 10 percent of all employees and less than 25 percent of managers were trained in VBM concepts.

More seriously, however, the company failed to make significant changes in its processes. Budgeting and strategic planning systems remained separate from each other. The company continued to fund individual projects coming up through the system, basing funding decisions largely on the reputation of the sponsoring managers and on the perceived fit of a project with the CEO's vision. And for good measure, senior management interfered frequently in the resource allocation process, suggesting that politicking and gaming were rife.

As one might expect, this company reported in our survey that it took no important actions based on VBM and that, far from having a positive impact on employees' behavior, its VBM program actually had a negative effect. Eventually, the company abandoned its VBM program, declaring the experiment a failure.

The featured CEOs will also discuss the challenges they faced in building an ownership culture and the pitfalls that await companies when the right organizational conditions are not put in place.

1. THE GOVERNING OBJECTIVE OF THE COMPANY

Back in Chapter 2 we emphasized the importance of establishing the right governing objective for the corporation. We are not going to reprise the entire discussion, but there are a few points worth highlighting.

Consistent decisions across time and businesses require a consistent governing objective. Why? Because multiple objectives lead to contradictions and inconsistent choices over time.

There is a common belief among many CEOs that no single objective is appropriate for all businesses, at all times, and in all situations. They feel they must have the flexibility to determine what performance objective should be emphasized in any given business at any given point in time. While this may seem sensible on the surface, history has repeatedly shown that it is not the way to go.

To illustrate this point, let's consider one all too common example. The stated goal of a well known Fortune 200 chief executive was "to achieve global leadership." Responding to this goal, his management team pursued an all-out effort to expand the global footprint of the company and capture a greater share of worldwide sales. Give credit to the management team: the company was able to achieve its stated objective within a few years, with the help of a few large acquisitions. However, the company was still not the leading player in a few large and growing regions of the world, especially in China, where despite healthy revenue growth the company was losing share. Shortly thereafter, the CEO challenged management: "Why are you going after revenue growth all over the globe? You need to focus on gaining share in China." So management stopped focusing on increasing global sales and began increasing the size of its sales and distribution network in China. Shortly thereafter, the analyst community began highlighting the lower operating margins that the company was delivering relative to its primary competitor. So the directive came down to: "Get your operating margins back in line with the competition!" And so management began cutting SG&A expense. And yes, you guessed it, growth and capital returns began to decline and the company's shareholder returns suffered.

In contrast, the CEO of the primary competitor consistently reminded his team that their ultimate objective was to capture the greatest share of global economic profits. It was up to the business managers to identify those markets with the largest and fastest growing economic profit pools and to focus their strategies and resources on capturing a leading share of those economically attractive markets. As a result, the competitor captured the majority of the industry's global economic profit growth and tripled its shareholder value over a seven-year period, far exceeding the shareholder returns of its rival.

Without a single governing objective, management is unable to consistently manage the trade-offs between competing objectives—growing revenues, improving margins, and realizing returns above the cost of capital.

What Is the "Right" Governing Objective?

There are any number of financial, strategic, and institutional objectives a company might adopt. Some of the choices are listed in Figure 6.2.

Financial Objectives	Strategic Objectives	Institutional Objectives
• Revenue Growth	• Share Leadership	• Excellence, Greatness
• EPS Growth	• Size, Scope Advantage	• Reputation, Admiration
• Return on Capital Targets	• Quality Advantage	• Survival, Staying Power
• Minimize "Risk" or Earnings Volatility	• Brand Equity Advantage	• Stable Employment

Figure 6.2: Potential Governing Objectives

However, there are inherent problems associated with using any of these metrics as an ultimate measure of success or criterion for making trade-off decisions, because none of these metrics reflect performance in both the customer market and the capital markets.

There is only one measure that consistently defines success in both the customer *and* capital markets, and that is the company's share and growth of economic profits. All other measures of performance impact the business's share of economic profits.

Finally, some will react negatively to the term "maximize," as in "maximize shareholder value growth." The term seems to be antithetical to stability and prudence. However, we have found the term to be important. Unless management is constantly challenged to make decisions that deliver the *greatest possible economic profit growth over time*, they will not deliver superior shareholder returns. This does not imply that businesses should manage for the short-term; after all, shareholder value creation, as you know, is driven by the discounted value of long-term economic profit growth. But the statement does not negate the fact that management should never be satisfied with lower sustainable economic profit growth than is possible.

> "While the difference between creating and maximizing value may seem subtle, it is a very profound difference that drives a much broader examination of strategic and resource allocation alternatives."
>
> —Travis Engen, former Chief Executive, ITT Industries and Alcan Aluminum

What naturally follows from establishing one common governing objective?

- The corporate center and every business unit should have targets for the level of economic profit growth they are trying to achieve.
- Major strategic and resource allocation decisions should be made by selecting the alternative that is most likely to maximize economic profit growth over time.

Now let's move on to how the roles and responsibilities of the corporate center, business units, and functional units impact a company's ability to effectively manage shareholder value.

2. ROLES AND RESPONSIBILITIES

A clear definition of roles and responsibilities, and a corresponding alignment of individual decision authority and performance accountability, is essential in any corporation, business, or functional support unit.

The Executive Center

There are four roles that only the CEO (with the aid of the executive team) can perform. Only the CEO can define the:

1. Governing objective and ultimate measure of success for the corporation.
2. Value-improvement agenda for the corporation.
3. Organizational boundaries that define the units for which strategies will be developed, resources will be allocated, and performance will be monitored and managed.
4. Standards and processes by which strategies will be approved, resources will be allocated, and performance will be managed.

Sir Brian Pitman, former Chairman and Chief Executive of Lloyds TSB, summarized the role of the corporate executive center well in a slide he used to address his organization. (See Figure 6.3.)

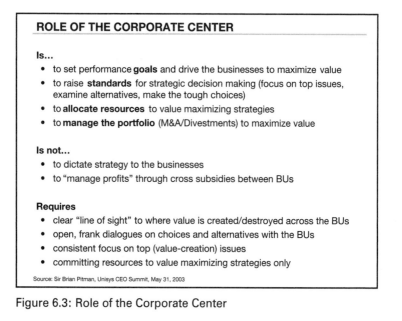

Figure 6.3: Role of the Corporate Center

The Business Unit

Similarly, there are certain roles that are best performed by business unit management. Since the business unit managers are closest to— and therefore better understand—the customers and competitors, they are in the best position to formulate and recommend business unit strategies for approval and resourcing. And once the strategy is approved, only the business unit is in the position to manage the execution of that strategy.

Therefore the unique roles and responsibilities of the business unit are to:

1. Develop a factual understanding of market economics and competitive position.

2. Formulate and evaluate strategic alternatives and recommend the highest-value strategy to the executive center for modification or approval.

3. Translate the strategy into detailed implementation plans.

Functional Support Units

Functional support units can be very important, but no matter how important they are, they are not businesses. Functional units are critical to setting and administering corporate standards (including corporate reporting standards, human resources standards, and legal and regulatory standards), and corporate support services (such as supply chain and R&D management) can have a significant impact on business unit performance. However, none of these functional units produce economic profits, so they cannot have strategies that are independent of the business units they support.

Therefore, the primary roles of functional support units are to:

1. Improve the efficiency or effectiveness of a functional activity, in support of one or more business units.
2. Transfer best-demonstrated practices across one or more business units.

The executive center, the business units, and the functional support groups play unique roles in managing and increasing economic profit growth.

Yet each of these organizational units can also act in ways that detract from economic profit growth and shareholder value.

The executive center can:

- Set corporate goals or objectives that are inconsistent with maximizing shareholder value.
- Make portfolio investment strategies, like value-consuming acquisitions, that fail to recapture the cost of investment.
- Generate overhead expense in excess of their contribution to the efficiency and effectiveness of the businesses.

Business units can:

- Pursue strategies or allocate resources in a way that does not maximize their economic profit growth.
- "Game" the budget and resource allocation process by undercommitting to near-term targets while overestimating longer-term growth.

Functional support units can:

- Unilaterally pursue functional objectives without input or coordination with the business units, thus ultimately detracting from maximizing economic profit growth.

3. BUSINESS BOUNDARIES

The way business boundaries are drawn has a significant influence on a corporation's ability to manage economic profit growth. After all, business boundaries determine the units for which strategies will be developed, resources will be allocated, and performance will be measured and managed. The best structure a corporation can adopt is the one that creates the greatest transparency and accountability for economic profit growth.

Yet, few organizational structures have been designed with that objective in mind. Instead, business boundaries are often established to achieve the "right" number of direct reports, simplify corporate reporting, or achieve cost synergies. These alternative goals are not harmful in and of themselves but they can lead to unintended consequences.

There are four common mistakes companies make in defining business boundaries:

1. Defining a business boundary too broadly
2. Defining a business boundary too narrowly
3. Creating consolidated functional silos
4. Assuming a matrix structure solves your problems

Defining Business Boundaries Too Broadly: The Alcan Story

A common mistake is to define organizational boundaries around more than one economically independent performance unit. As a result, the concentration of economic profits in a business is not recognized or managed and the strategy of the business is, by definition, too broad.

Let's discuss the real-life example Travis Engen encountered when he took over the leadership of Alcan in 2001.

Alcan had been a long-term underperformer in the aluminum industry, as you can see in Figure 6.4, which shows the company's economic growth and shareholder returns compared with its primary competitor, Alcoa.

Alcan had been organized and managed as four separate divisions:

1. **Bauxite mining and refining.** This division was responsible for refining bauxite, a naturally occurring clay compound rich in alumina (the source mineral from which the element aluminum is extracted). Within the division, operations were monitored and managed by the mining location where the refining assets were also located.

2. **Primary metals.** This division was responsible for extracting or "smelting" aluminum from the mineral alumina. Smelting is an energy-intensive process, and Alcan owned and managed extensive hydro-energy assets, which produced the bulk of the power needed for the processes. Prior management had lumped the energy assets into the Primary Metals division. Both hydroelectric energy production and smelting activities require enormous amounts of capital investment. Alcan managed these operations by production facility.

3. **Rolled products.** This division was responsible for rolling, pressing, and casting aluminum into a multitude of products

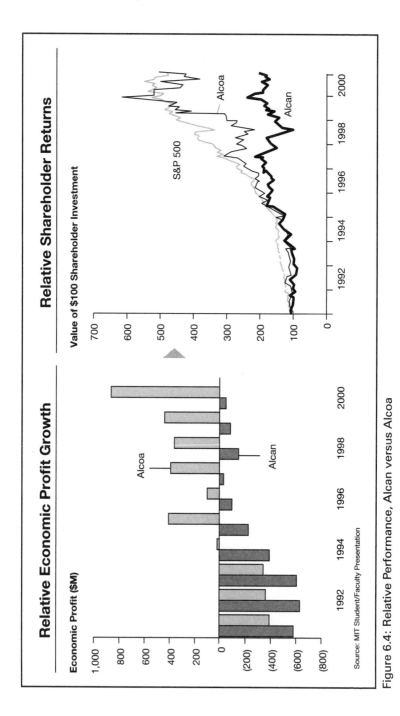

Figure 6.4: Relative Performance, Alcan versus Alcoa

sold to customers across a range of industries. As in the Primary Metals division, rolling and fabrication operations were monitored and managed by a production facility, and resources were allocated to facility-specific projects.

4. *Packaging products.* The packaging division produced a range of paper, plastic, film, and aluminum foil packaging products for a diverse set of end markets across a wide array of industries. Unlike the other divisions, the Packaging Products division was further broken down into end market business units, each having control over its own production, marketing, sales, and distribution operations.

Figure 6.5 shows the economic profit generated by each of the Alcan divisions.

Throughout the history of the company, Alcan had been pursuing a fully integrated strategy, to drive aluminum demand through the sale of its fabricated products.

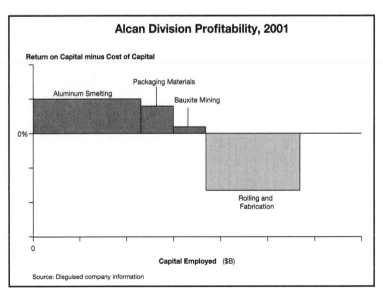

Figure 6.5: Economic Profits Generated by Alcan's Four Divisions

This strategy of balanced supply and demand was keeping facility utilizations high, and, as a result, Alcan was one of the most efficient producers of aluminum in the industry. Yet Alcan had lower economic profit margins relative to its leading competitor, Alcoa.

An analysis of the operating and strategic differences between Alcan and Alcoa revealed that the margin differences between these two competitors were not the result of differences in production efficiencies but rather differences in business mix. Alcoa was not focused on balancing upstream supply with downstream demand. They considered each step of the production process as a separate business with independent strategies and P&L responsibilities. Alcoa's mining, smelting, and fabrication divisions were each free to produce more or less volume than the downstream Alcoa division demanded. They were also free to sell their output to other companies worldwide. Similarly, Alcoa's downstream divisions were free to purchase their supply needs from other aluminum companies. In doing so, Alcoa increased the degrees of freedom and strategic options available to each division.

Alcoa's divisions were also organized differently than the Alcan divisions. For example, Alcan's fabrication division was organized and managed by a production facility, while Alcoa's fabrication division was separated into end-market business units. Each Alcoa end-market unit was responsible for its own revenue, costs, and capital usage. As a result of this organizational structure, Alcoa managers were better able to recognize and act on the wide variation in economic profit margins and growth potential across the many different fabrication and rolled product end markets.

At Alcan, all rolled product volume was viewed as good volume because it increased facility utilization and lowered the company's average cost per pound, while Alcoa's business unit structure caused management to focus on profitability per pound. As a result, more resources were devoted to producing profitable aerospace products, and fewer resources were devoted to producing non-differentiated automotive products.

One of the first things Engen did after he assumed the role of chief executive in 2001 was conduct an in-depth financial and strategic assessment of the corporate portfolio. That assessment revealed more than 23 economically independent Alcan performance units embedded within the corporation's four divisions. The divisional structure and focus on minimizing costs, as opposed to maximizing profitability, was preventing management from seeing and acting on the concentration of economic profits that existed within each division and across the end-markets they served.

Armed with an improved understanding of business economics, Engen quickly reorganized the corporation into 23 separate, economically independent business units. This reorganization opened up new strategic and resource allocation opportunities that had not previously been apparent or possible.

Over the course of the next three years, Alcan:

- Invested in the expansion of its power business.
- Dramatically expanded its global bauxite mining and refining business, becoming one of the world's largest producers of alumina.
- Invested in new organic smelting capacity while also acquiring two large European companies with quality smelting assets.
- Spun off its economically unprofitable rolled-products division into a new publicly traded company (Novelis).
- Acquired a range of companies that were well positioned in attractive segments of the primary aluminum and packaging markets.

As a result of these portfolio changes and further refinements in business unit strategies (see Figure 6.6), Alcan significantly improved

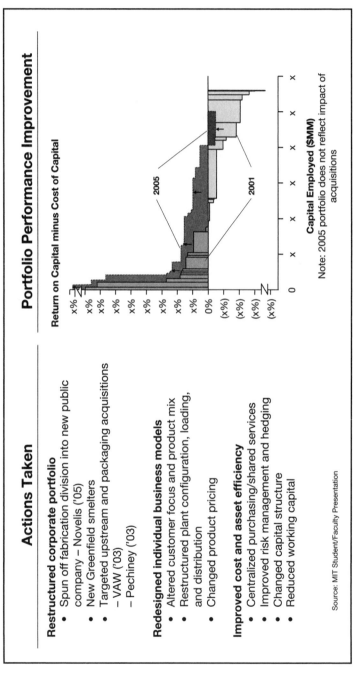

Figure 6.6: Alcan Divisional Performance Improvement, 2001–2005

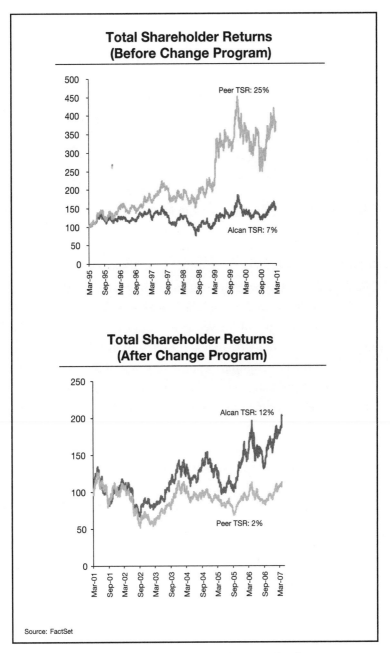

Figure 6.7: Improvement in Alcan's Total Shareholder Returns

economic profit growth and total shareholder returns, outpacing Alcoa and the rest of the aluminum competitors. (See Figure 6.7.)

Under the previous organizational structure, this kind of change would not have been possible. Only after disaggregating the corporation into separate, economically independent business units was management able to recognize the concentration of economic profits and develop and deploy the strategies to unlock the company's latent value-improvement potential.

Defining Business Boundaries Too Narrowly: The Coca-Cola Story

If businesses are defined too narrowly, the economic and strategic interdependencies between businesses can be mismanaged.

This had been the case at The Coca-Cola Company. Historically, the production and marketing of Coca-Cola products was the responsibility of Coca-Cola, while the sale and distribution of these products in the U.S. was the responsibility of over seventy independently owned and managed bottling franchises. This business structure had been in existence since the founding of the company over 125 years ago and served the company well as long as the majority of U.S. retailers, Coca-Cola's customers, were local or regional in scope. However, as the U.S. retail market increasingly consolidated into national chains, this business structure became increasingly inefficient.

It was just not possible to execute an integrated strategy for servicing the company's largest national customers. As a result, service quality and profitability began to suffer. Finally, the situation became so untenable that Coca-Cola began acquiring control of the major bottlers and improving joint strategic planning with the independent bottlers that remained.

This is an example of how business structure needs to evolve with changes in market structure. If business boundaries are defined too narrowly, the economic and strategic interdependencies among separate pieces of an integrated business cannot be well managed.

Creating Consolidated Functional Silos: The Rohm and Haas Story

See if this sounds familiar: at some point someone—a consultant perhaps—comes to top management and says, "You've got a very big operation here with a lot of complexity. If you consolidate your organization around core activities, like the supply-chain management and commercial operations, you will become more efficient and save a lot of money."

And so the corporation consolidates supply-chain management for a number of businesses into a single corporate-wide functional division. As a result, the company does realize meaningful cost savings and gross margins improve. However, as a by-product, the ability to measure and manage profitability at a granular level is compromised. The commercial unit is now focused on managing price and volume while the supply-chain organization is focused on managing costs and assets.

Of course, one of the easiest ways to decrease standard costs is to increase volume and production-facility utilization, and since the commercial organization is rewarded on revenue growth, they are all too happy to comply. A few years later, even though the company has improved average production efficiencies, average gross margins begin to decline. Why? Because the company has increased its mix of lower priced, lower margin volume. Since profitability can now only be measured and managed at an aggregate level, management has lost its ability to distinguish between profitable and unprofitable volume.

This is exactly what happened to Rohm and Haas's (R&H's) Performance Polymers business in the mid-1990s. Back then, the division was facing increases in raw material and energy costs that it was unable to fully pass along to its customers. As a result, margins declined, demand slowed, and R&H's shareholder returns suffered.

In an effort to improve margins, management consolidated the manufacturing and supply-chain operations of many of its business units into one global organization. Supply-chain management assumed responsibility for capacity and cost management, while the commercial units assumed responsibility for revenue growth.

Initially, the consolidation was considered a tremendous success, as redundant operating costs were taken out of the company. Growth increased and the company began expanding production capacity. For the next couple of years, things seemed to be headed in the right direction. But by the third year, margins again began to decline and the company's shareholder returns began to lag behind its competition. This time, however, it was not being driven by increases in input costs.

As things continued to get progressively worse for Rohm and Haas but not for its competitors, the corporation decided to conduct an in-depth financial and strategic assessment of its businesses to better understand the sources and drivers of its margin disadvantage. Management was surprised to learn that more than 50 percent of the Performance Polymers division's businesses had become economically unprofitable. A large percentage of the top-line growth it had achieved over the past five years was consuming shareholder value. (See Figure 6.8.)

Because the company had separated responsibility for revenue and cost management, transparency and accountability for managing profits had decreased. Under a functional structure, all revenues looked attractive, because they increased facility utilization and lowered blended standard costs.

When both the commercial and supply-chain organizations are incented to grow volume—one to meet its revenue targets, and the other to improve facility utilization and reduce aggregate standard costs—you can be sure volume will increase. And with increased volume come capacity constraints and the need for additional capital investment. In the case of R&H's Performance Polymers business, the net result was the destruction of shareholder value. (See Figure 6.9.)

Operating Groups	Business Units	Operating Margin	Economic Profit ($M)
Group 1	1A	13%	$270M
	1B	18%	260
	1C	11%	140
	1D	12%	10
	1E	26%	10
Group 2	2A	11%	30
	2B	14%	20
	2C	17%	10
	2D	4%	(60)
	2E	(5%)	(100)
Group 3	3A	7%	0
	3B	8%	(10)
	3C	4%	(60)
	3D	7%	(70)
Group 4	4A	7%	(40)
	4B	6%	(10)
	4C	7%	(10)
	4D	2%	(90)
	4E	3%	(200)
Group 5	5A	7%	(30)
			$130M

Financial Figures Disguised
Source: MIT Student/Faculty Presentation

Figure 6.8: Economic Profits at Rohm and Haas's Performance Polymers Division

Once R&H understood what was going on, then-COO Mike Fitzpatrick reorganized the Performance Polymers business into individual business units, each with responsibility and authority to

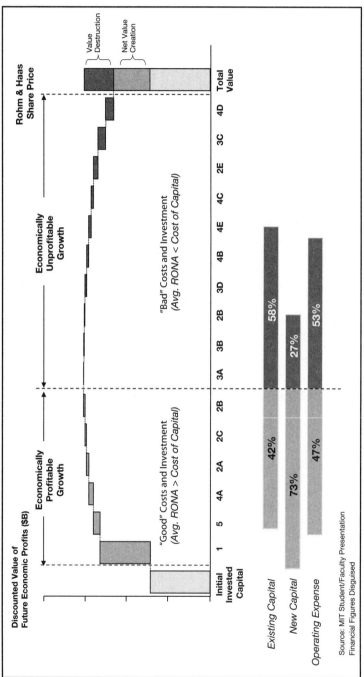

Figure 6.9: Profitable and Unprofitable Growth at Rohm and Haas

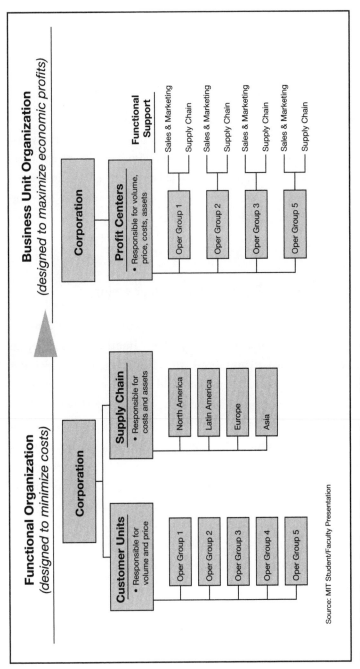

Figure 6.10: Organizational Changes at Rohm and Haas

manage the revenues, costs, investments and therefore the economic profits of their business. (See Figure 6.10.)

Functional responsibility for managing shared production assets remained, but business unit managers now had the authority to challenge capital investments and cost allocations and were free to seek sourcing alternatives to in-house production.

As a result of this restructuring, the Performance Polymers division was again able to see where and why economic profits were concentrated, and this renewed transparency led to several changes in division strategy and resource allocation. As a result, R&H was able to restore economically profitable growth to Performance Polymers division, and significantly improved the company's shareholder returns.

Assuming a Matrix Structure Solves Your Problems

Almost all businesses need to manage interdependencies between product, customer, and regional segments. In other words, they are inherently matrixed organizations. Therefore it would seem logical to create a matrixed structure, with a head of product management, a head of customer or sales management, and a head of each regional market. However, a matrixed structure alone does not answer the fundamental question: who is ultimately accountable for economic profit growth?

Some companies answer that question by measuring profitability along each dimension of the matrix and holding the product, customer, and regional heads accountable for profit growth along that dimension. But that still does not answer the question: who is accountable for managing the strategic trade-offs that occur in deciding where and how to compete? For example, if the product manager does not want to offer an unprofitable product, but the customer manager considers that product necessary to secure the broader profitable customer relationship, who gets to decide?

Matrixed organizations are a necessary reality in many businesses. To ignore product, customer, and regional interdependencies would severely compromise performance. However, one dimension of the matrix must be given ultimate authority for making trade-off decisions and be held accountable for the economic profit implications of these decisions. Said another way, there is always one dimension of the matrix that should trump the others when it comes to making strategic and resource allocation decisions. In most cases, decisions about which customers to serve and how to serve them will have the greatest impact on the sustainable economic profit growth of a business; therefore, it is usually the customer dimension of the matrix that should have ultimate strategic decision authority.

Final Comment on Business Boundaries

It is a common refrain that structure follows strategy; however, as illustrated in earlier examples, the way business boundaries are defined can have a tremendous impact on a company's ability to see where and why economic profits are concentrated and therefore decide what strategies should be employed to improve economic profit growth. Business boundaries should be designed with the explicit goal of creating the greatest transparency and accountability for managing economic profit growth.

4. DECISION STANDARDS AND PROCESSES

Establishing the right governing objective, roles and responsibilities, and business boundaries goes a long way to promoting the right behavior, but that is not enough to ensure that strategic, resource allocation, and performance management decisions are aligned with shareholder interest. Companies also need to establish the standards for how these decisions will be made. Specifically:

- What information do we need to make these decisions?
- What criteria will we use to make those decisions?
- What processes will we use to build the understanding, commitment, and follow-through required to make those decisions a reality?

Top management may not feel they need to specify these standards to arrive at good decisions. However, as we discussed earlier, a lot of shareholder value is created or destroyed by decisions made at the business unit level. So it is very helpful to set standards and expectations for the rest of the organization to follow. To state the obvious, you are likely to find that your interactions with the business units are much more productive if you do.

Strategic Decision Standards and Processes

The objective of any business strategy is to define *where* and *how* the business will compete to create customer and shareholder value. As discussed in Chapter 5, in order to achieve that objective, the strategy-development process should involve:

1. *Fact-based assessment* of economic profit concentrations, customer needs, market economics, and competitive position. In other words, what are the fundamental drivers of the business's economic profits in each served market?

2. *Consideration of strategic alternatives* to address the highest value-at-stake issues and opportunities. In other words, what changes in market participation, offer (including promotion), pricing, or operating configuration should be considered, and which set of integrated strategic choices will deliver the greatest economic profit growth?

3. *Translating decisions into implementation plans and commitments.* There is a big gap between agreeing on a strategy and delivering the results it promises. Unless strategies are translated into performance commitments, resource requirements, and specific actions and time lines, they will become decoupled from budgets and day-to-day priorities, and it will become impossible to monitor and manage the implementation over time. (See Chapter 5.)

Unless they are informed about the economics of the markets in which the business unit competes, and the unit's competitive position in those markets, senior management will be confined to driving business performance through top-down targets set to achieve incremental improvements over last year's performance. In such cases, unfortunately, negotiations of annual budget targets typically replace well-informed discussions of strategic alternatives.

Why? Because there is not enough interaction between the business units and corporate executive team during the strategic decision-making process. When this is the case, it is very challenging for top management to truly understand the opportunities and limitations the business units face.

As a result, top management does not really understand how a business unit will make its numbers, while the business units are often forced to take actions that may jeopardize long-term performance in order to hit each year's ever-escalating target.

To bring this discussion to a close, and to tie it back to what we discussed in Chapter 5, let us remind you of what the best CEOs repeatedly told us: even though responsibility for formulating and recommending business unit strategies rests with the managers of those units, there should be substantive dialogue between the units and the executive management team at each of the three stages of the strategy-decision process.

Resource Allocation Decision Standards and Process

Resources should be allocated to business strategies, not projects.

How often have you approved a series of projects, all with internal rates of return over 20 percent, only to find that the business is still delivering a 7-percent overall return on capital? The problem is that projects are not businesses. No matter how good an individual project may appear on paper, if it is implemented within a business that is competitively disadvantaged in an unprofitable market, the return on the project and the overall business will remain unattractive.

So the evaluation of individual projects does little to help management better allocate resources. Instead, the projects that are required to implement a specific business strategy should be defined and approved within the context of the overall business strategy review and approval process.

Then, as the business meets its interim performance commitments, project funding can be distributed. Obviously, if interim performance targets are missed, an overall review of the business strategy is needed, and the associated projects that are part of implementing that strategy should be reconsidered.

What we are saying is that you need to set up a gated disbursement of incremental funds, and a periodic zero-based assessment of total capital invested. It is not enough to evaluate incremental capital distributions if a business is consistently missing its performance commitments and generating an economic loss. In such cases, the reallocation of embedded capital, as well as incremental capital, should be considered.

There should be zero tolerance for the continuation of value-consuming investments. Business managers must convince corporate management their strategy will contribute to economic profits within a reasonable period of time or resources should flow to other businesses that can deliver economically profitable growth.

Performance Monitoring and Management Standards and Process

One thing is certain: plans and forecasts, no matter how well developed, will always turn out to be imprecise predictors of the future. Businesses will inevitably face unforeseen execution problems or changes in market conditions and competitor actions. In some cases these changes can pose a significant risk to the future economic profit potential of the business. Therefore, the standards and processes for monitoring and managing performance should be no less disciplined than those you use for strategy development.

A disciplined performance management process should achieve three principle objectives:

1. Monitor variances in actual versus plan commitments:
   - Variances in actions taken versus plan
   - Variances in operating and financial results versus plan

2. Monitor changes in the external environment:
   - Changes in market economics
   - Changes in competitive position

3. Identify and resolve internal or external causes of variances, due to either:
   - Internal organizational impediments
   - External changes in market conditions

Obviously, if the variances could have a material impact on the economic profit and shareholder value of the corporation, the CEO and the executive team need to be informed of the facts, alternatives, and implementation requirements associated with those alternatives as the situation develops.

This is why the best value-managed companies establish a periodic, CEO-led, strategic performance review process. These reviews generally occur quarterly and focus on the highest value-at-stake issues and opportunities. The business units that are facing material strategic and operating variances are asked to provide an updated, fact-based set of alternatives and recommendations to be discussed with senior management. Following agreement on a course of action, the implementation details are subsequently submitted for approval, and performance monitoring begins with a renewed set of commitments.

When a quarterly strategic performance review process is in place, there is at most a three-month lag between the occurrence of underperformance and decisions about the strategic or organizational changes that will be taken to address the variance. As a result, the company avoids a lingering disconnect between the business strategy, budget commitments, and resource disbursements.

In effect, the annual strategic-planning process is replaced with rolling quarterly strategic performance reviews that focus on both monitoring performance versus plan and identifying new opportunities to improve economic profit growth.

It makes no sense either to delay addressing a material issue until the annual strategy development process begins or to ask businesses that are on track to meet their three-year plan to go through a new strategy-development process each year.

Essential Information

The organizations that are best at delivering shareholder value growth have aligned the standards and processes for setting targets, making strategic and resource allocation decisions, and monitoring and managing performance with the overall objective of maximizing economic profit growth. These standards and processes:

- Produce an informed executive center.

- Delegate authority while maintaining strict accountability.
- Result in fact-based decisions.

The information required to effectively manage shareholder value is shown in Figure 6.11.

Looking at this list will no doubt bring to mind the information companies do not collect or utilize. For example:

- When it comes to *setting targets*, most companies do not have an understanding of the expectations already reflected in their current stock price or the economic profit growth that will likely be required to deliver top quartile shareholder returns.

- When it comes to *strategy development*, most companies do not have an understanding of the total economic profits available in the markets or market segments they serve or what is driving their share of those profits.

- When it comes to *resource allocation*, information on both the progress and performance of major investment programs often is not available. And so when performance is finally reviewed, management can be surprised by just how far off track the return on investment has gotten.

- And when it comes to *performance management*, most review discussions are overly focused on financial outcomes, complete with detailed breakdowns of aggregate line item variances but devoid of business segment performance measures. Furthermore, most business reviews focus on what has happened in the past instead of what trends are occurring that will impact future performance. Seldom do performance reviews include a fact-based and informed discussion of the changes in market economics, customer needs, and competitor actions that are causing performance variances.

These information shortcomings exist despite an overwhelming number of management reports. We recall one company, a large producer of industrial products, whose management conducted an audit of all the management reports they received, some daily, some weekly, some monthly, and others quarterly. We asked senior management to keep a copy of every new report over a six-month period.

At the end of the six months, all the managers brought in their stacks of paper—one production executive actually wheeled in four boxes on a dolly.

We also asked them to show us the reports they felt were key to running the business. One executive pulled out a single 8-1/2 x 11 sheet of paper containing key profitability and operating statistics, and a page from his three-year strategic plan. He said, "All I need are these two pieces of paper. One contains what we said we were going do over three years, and the other answers how we are doing quarter to quarter."

Many executives tend to think of information gaps as a technology problem. So when you start talking about the issues, the people in IT will say they need a $100-million system upgrade to make the problems go away. But as we mentioned in Chapter 2, this sort of problem is rarely an IT problem. Odds are you can fix these information gaps without changing your systems. Often what is required is simply hiring a few analysts.

We aren't trying to be flip. We are trying to underscore something that you already know. The starting point in addressing your information gaps is to sit down with a sheet of paper and map out the answers to three general questions:

1. What information is required when, and at what levels of the organization, for each core decision process (target setting, strategic decision making, resource allocation, and performance management)?
2. Where is that information?
3. How will it be gathered, processed, analyzed, and reported?

Target Setting	Strategy Development	Resource Allocation	Performance Management
• Peer group companies • Historical total shareholder returns of peer companies • Analyst forecasts of company's future earnings growth and return on capital • Calculation of corporate cash flow and economic profit growth, which, when discounted to present value, approximates the recent stock price • Roll-up of management's business unit and corporate financial forecast	• Market sizes, growth, average profit margins, and capital returns • Historical and forecasted trends in economic profit margins and growth and key drivers of changes (e.g., changes in relative power of buyers and sellers, regulatory or government policy changes, level of competitive intensity, new technological innovations, etc.) • Relative economic profit margin and growth of each major business unit v.s. its competition • Major business model differences between each major business unit and their competition (i.e., differences in participation, offer, pricing, or operating configuration) • Highest value-at-stake issues and opportunities facing each major business unit and the corporation	• Current allocation of all invested capital • Current allocation of management resources • Economic profit being generated per dollar of invested capital • Prioritization of incremental capital requests based on discounted value of economic profit growth associated with those incremental investments • Performance milestones for interim distribution of incremental capital • Capital investment performance audits	• Implementation plans (including actions, accountabilities, and interim operating and financial performance targets by business unit and relevant business unit segment • Quarterly performance reports with variance to operating and financial targets and recommendations for addressing variance • Periodic strategic performance review sessions where performance is evaluated relative to plan commitments and the economic profit/shareholder-value-improvement agenda is refreshed

Figure 6.11: Typical Set of Metrics Used by Top Value-Managed Companies

Only then should you consider what systems changes may be needed to automate the information processing and reporting. If new IT resources are needed, you add them. But that isn't where you begin. You begin with that sheet of paper. Information planning must precede information technology.

5. INCENTIVE PRACTICES

The ultimate objective of an incentive compensation system is to encourage behavior that is aligned with the organization's objectives and strategies. However, many companies have failed in their efforts to achieve this alignment.

Only a fraction of incentive systems are tied to profit growth and shareholder performance. And when they are, rewards are seldom proportional to performance. How many times have you witnessed similar rewards for widely different levels of performance? The answer: countless.

That isn't surprising. For example, it has been well documented that CEO compensation, to pick one example that's especially close to home, is not generally well correlated with companies' total shareholder return performance. (See Figure 6.12.)

On the surface, that doesn't make sense. Why don't share-price incentive schemes lead to better shareholder performance growth? The reasons are varied, but let's discuss two briefly:

1. First, absolute share-price performance does a poor job of distinguishing between the performance of companies within an industry. Equity values are impacted, often to a large degree, by macro-trends that affect all industry competitors. For example, when political unrest in the Middle East threatens oil supply and oil prices increase, all companies in the oil industry tend to do well. Similarly, during and after the recent financial meltdown, all bank and brokerage stocks were hammered.

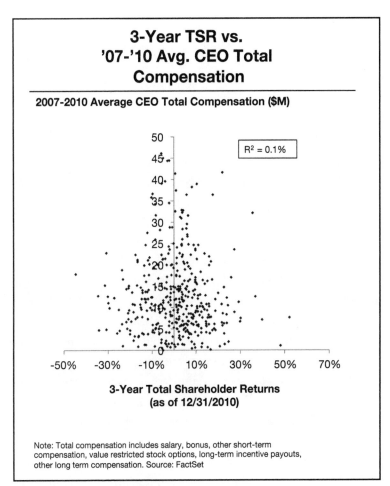

3-Year TSR vs. '07-'10 Avg. CEO Total Compensation

2007-2010 Average CEO Total Compensation ($M)

$R^2 = 0.1\%$

3-Year Total Shareholder Returns (as of 12/31/2010)

Note: Total compensation includes salary, bonus, other short-term compensation, value restricted stock options, long-term incentive payouts, other long term compensation. Source: FactSet

Figure 6.12: The Correlation Between CEO Compensation and Total Shareholder Returns Is Poor

2. Restricted share or option awards are the result of negotiations between the board's compensation committee, executive-compensation advisors and management. This process rarely results in incentive schemes where rewards are proportional to the relative performance of a company within an industry. Stories abound about CEOs who continue to receive huge paychecks even though shareholders suffer.

To eliminate these problems, we have a simple suggestion: tie top management's compensation to the shareholder returns a company delivers relative to its peers and/or link executive compensation to the company's growth in economic profits relative to its peers.

Line-Management Incentives

Intriguingly, stock ownership is not a very effective means of motivating line managers. Why? Because line managers seldom have the span of influence needed to affect the shareholder returns of the entire company. Sure, if their business unit does well, it helps the company's overall performance. But the company likely has lots of business units, and so the individual manager's impact is small.

To influence behavior, line manager rewards need to be more closely aligned with a manager's sphere of influence and the performance of their business unit. To align behavior with shareholder interest, line management incentives should be driven by the economic profit growth their business generates.

That's just common sense. Yet most line management incentive plans are a collection of conflicting revenue, share, and operating profit growth targets that actually constrain the strategic options a business can consider.

While there is no one-size-fits-all approach to aligning compensation and incentives, there are some common principles found in all effective shareholder-focused line management incentive compensation systems. The systems:

- Motivate the behavior that drives economically profitable growth.

- Result in total compensation that attracts and retains the talent needed to effectively execute the right business strategies.

- Provide variable compensation that is not capped and is proportional to an individual's contribution to the realized economic profit growth.

That last point, as BB&T's John Allison explains, is only rational. "Those who contribute the most should receive the most," he says. "Now, you have to measure that contribution. Those large payments have to be earned. But if we have people who have contributed disproportionately to our success, they should be paid accordingly. At one point as CEO, I was the forty-fifth highest-paid person at BB&T. And I have to tell you, I was extremely happy about that outcome. First of all, I was being paid a lot. But more important, all those people who were making more than me were making me look good, through their contribution to our performance. The ones I worried about were the people who weren't making more than me but should have been. Were they hurting our performance?"

How Well Did You Do?

When Jim Kilts took over as CEO of Gillette, he asked each global business unit and functional manager two questions: what did they view as their primary responsibility and accountability? And how well did they think they were fulfilling it?

"The answer to the second question was always the same. They always told me, 'I have performed my role very well.'"

And yet, between 1999 and 2000, Gillette's sales and profit growth was zero. In fact, Gillette had been struggling since 1995. The only thing Kilts could figure out was that these managers were judging themselves on effort. But given the results, you couldn't say they were doing their jobs well.

"Effort that does not turn into results is not good job performance," Kilts says.

Things changed in a hurry after his appointment as CEO. Within a year, sixty-six of the top one hundred positions were filled either with Gillette employees who were new to their positions or in some cases with outside hires.

In thinking about how to re-staff the organization, Kilts had three overarching ideas in mind:

1. He knew the skills, capabilities, and attributes Gillette needed as a whole.
2. He decided which skills, capabilities, and attributes were needed for each key position, and he made sure the person placed there would be a good fit. "The best and brightest 'square peg' will never be a star performer in a 'round hole,'" he says. (And, of course, putting the best people in positions that have the greatest potential impact on the organization is another example of putting a disproportionate amount of resources against your largest opportunities.)
3. He made sure the sum of the skills, capabilities, and attributes in the key positions covered all of the company's important needs.

Not only did many of the people in key positions change, but the way these managers were evaluated changed as well. Each manager was objectively evaluated on results achieved against a five-point scale that covered agreed-upon business and personal objectives. Meeting or just barely exceeding the stretch targets would only get a rating of 3—"meets expectations."

And to make sure that they knew what was expected, there was a dramatically increased emphasis on strategic and annual plans.

Just about every CEO has their business develop a strategic plan. Few do it with the rigor that Jim Kilts requires. The people who worked for him at Kraft, Nabisco, and Gillette recall the agonizing weeks on end they spent developing the facts, considering strategic alternatives, and translating their strategies into implementation commitments.

Kilts makes no apologies for working them that hard. Done right, he says, such business plans have five extremely tangible benefits:

1. They unify the company, since there is input and participation from every corner of the organization.
2. They provide the perfect dashboard with which to judge at a glance how well the company is doing, since growth in sales, earnings, market share, and the introduction of new products and economic profit growth are part of a good plan.
3. They are a source of motivation, since the targets in the plan, Kilts says, should be "tough enough to be challenging and cause the organization to stretch and grow. But they must be achievable so that everyone is fully engaged in the effort and feels accountable."
4. They underscore what's important. Simply setting the goals defining the priorities establishes what the company values.
5. They should be the basis for compensation and recognition. That lets everyone know how well they are doing and how they will be rewarded.

All this paid off shortly after the new evaluation and performance plan was implemented. Between 2003 and 2004, Gillette's sales climbed 13 percent, profits 23 percent, and EPS 25 percent. And the scores for managers? Some 74 percent got a 3, 19 percent scored "exceeds expectations," and only 4 percent got "outstanding." In other words, this kind of performance is what you are expected to do. You are rewarded for performance, not effort.

Details about the Corporate Incentive Plan

The kinds of incentive system that are most effective:

- Establish a framework for both objective and subjective performance-evaluation components.
- Are simple to understand, track, and administer.
- Are seen by management and employees as fair, predictable, and accurate.
- Are consistently applied across businesses and over time—they are stable and enduring.

There are other challenges to designing a performance-based incentive system. Some suggested approaches to dealing with those challenges are outlined in Figure 6.13.

Figure 6.13: Pitfalls and Solutions for Corporate Incentive Plans

Common Pitfalls	Solutions
Using the Wrong Measures of Performance	**Tie Incentives to Economic Profit Growth**
Revenue, EBITDA, or earnings per share alone do not drive stock price. The efficient use of capital to generate those revenues and earnings is also important.	A company's stock price is driven by investor expectations of future cash flows and economic profit.
Encouraging pursuit of one or more of the financial drivers listed above, without understanding their impact on economic profit growth, is just as likely to consume shareholder value as it is to create it.	Tying incentive rewards to economic profit growth creates a direct linkage between management and shareholder interests.

Continues on next page

Continued from previous page

Common Pitfalls	Solutions
Basing Incentives on Single-Period Performance Measures Incentives are often excessively dependent on single-period measures of performance; as a result, managers do not pay sufficient attention to long-term investment requirements and may even be encouraged to "game" short-term accounting.	**"Bank" a Portion of Annual Incentive Rewards and Defer Payout** Withhold a portion of annual incentive payouts. Deductions are made from the "banked" incentives when performance is below standard and/or when expected economic profits are not realized.
Rewarding Performance Outside an Employee's Sphere of Influence Corporate performance and value is comprised of many individual economic units. Understanding these independent units and aligning management incentives with each is fundamental to transparency and accountability. Awarding bonuses on performance that is outside an employee's control is like giving only one report card to a whole class of students: the best students will become demoralized and the worst ones will be thrilled to coast on everyone else's efforts.	**Tie the Majority of Incentives to the Performance for Which Employees Are Responsible** Corporate management should be rewarded for the economic profit growth of the entire company. Business unit managers should be mostly rewarded for the economic profit improvement of their businesses. Sales and other employees within businesses should be rewarded for their contribution to activities that generate economic profit, consistent with the unit's strategy. Managers of shared-services centers should be rewarded for the combined economic profit improvement of the units they support.

Continues on next page

Continued from previous page

Common Pitfalls	Solutions
Excessive Reliance on Stock Options and Grants Only corporate executives have the sphere of influence to directly impact overall corporate results. Options tend to reward the performance of the overall market, not the relative capital market performance of a company compared with its peers.	**Replace Stock and Stock-Option Grants with Economic Profit-Based Incentives** Limit large option and stock grants to corporate executives. When used, tie options or stock grants to relative shareholder value returns versus peers. Base the majority of performance-based compensation on economic profit performance.
Lack of Materiality, Capping the Upside, and Tying Incentives to Budget Targets Bonuses are not a cost to be minimized but rather a share of the performance improvement (value creation) to be maximized. The bigger and more concrete the incentive pay, the better for all concerned. Linking bonuses to budget targets generally encourages managers to set conservative, easy-to-achieve goals, transforming the entire budget process into an exercise in minimization.	**Tie Incentives to Economic Profit Growth** Bonuses should be structured as a share of performance improvements—that is, as a percentage of the additional wealth created.

Continues on next page

Continued from previous page

Creating Incentive Plans in Isolation of a Supporting Management Model	Design Incentive Plans as Part of an Integrated Approach to Manage Shareholder Value Growth
Incentive plans alone will not drive shareholder value improvement. Creating the incentive but not the ability to manage shareholder value growth is a recipe for failure.	Incentive compensation changes must be part of an integrated approach to managing the value of a company, which includes all the things we have talked about: • A clear definition of winning and internal measure of success • Granular understanding of sources and drivers of economic profit in each business • A quantified value-improvement agenda • Fundamental business model and resource allocation changes • Integrated performance management processes

Stages of Instituting a Shareholder Value Incentive System

How might a new incentive system be rolled out? Linking corporate executive incentives to economic profit growth and shareholder returns should happen early on. However, changes in line-management incentives should only occur after those managers have been shown how to improve economic profits, and after the corporation has the ability to credibly measure economic profit at the business unit level.

Changes to incentive plans should be part of an integrated improvement in management processes, that helps line managers understand what information is required to make good strategic choices; how strategic and resource allocation alternatives should be developed, decided upon, and implemented; and how performance should be monitored and managed going forward.

In working with many successful companies to change their incentive systems, as part of a comprehensive effort to better manage shareholder value, we have found the following sequence of actions to be successful:

1. First Six Months:

a. Develop understanding and agreement on the part of the executive committee regarding:

- The company's shareholder performance goals.
- The economic profit growth target required to achieve that goal, tying top management's compensation to multi-year economic profit and shareholder performance targets.

b. Develop a factual understanding of the sources and drivers of shareholder value in each line of business, as well as the strategic and resource alternatives for improving economic profit growth.

c. Identify and eliminate aspects of executive and line manager incentive that are causing value-destroying decisions. That means getting rid of:

- Too many conflicting metrics.
- Sales or share targets that encourage unprofitable growth.
- Indiscriminate cost savings or return on capital goals that compromise investment in profitable growth.

2. Next Six Months to Twelve Months:

a. Begin implementing the strategic and resource allocation changes.

b. Institute common information standards and processes for strategic, resource allocation, and performance management decisions across all business units.

c. Define and begin implementing an economic profit-based management compensation system across the company.

6. EDUCATION AND CAPABILITIES DEVELOPMENT

Most value-managed companies featured in this book have invested significantly more time and resources in training and developing their management talent than their competition has. How important do the best CEOs consider training to be? BB&T is one example.

"We have created our own university," says John Allison of BB&T. "Our education budget is 500 percent larger than what [our competitor] SunTrust spends, but we only spend 20 percent of what they do on advertising. Our theory is that it is all about word of mouth. The way we grow our business is by doing a great job for customers, and they tell their friends. And the only way you can do a good job is if you know what to do."

These companies also recognize that real learning comes from doing, and so their management development programs also tend to be more closely aligned with career progression planning.

The *Harvard Business Review* article we mentioned at the beginning of the chapter helps illustrate just how important this investment in capabilities development is to the long-term performance of a company.

Of the companies the INSEAD professors studied, those that focused on building management capabilities delivered much higher levels of sustainable shareholder returns than those that did not. (See Figure 6.14.)

Educating and Involving Your Board of Directors

The CEOs featured in this book have also spent considerable time communicating and educating their Boards of Directors.

Most directors of Fortune 500 companies are experienced and accomplished executives; however, they are not immune from holding misconceptions about what drives shareholder value and how to effectively manage its growth.

Effective CEOs appreciate that the level of strategic and organizational change often required to achieve and sustain superior shareholder returns cannot be accomplished without the understanding and support of their board. For this reason, the CEOs have devoted meaningful effort to discussing these concepts with their directors. They involve their boards in debate about the core beliefs and behaviors necessary to effectively manage shareholder value, and they actively involve their boards in a review of the highest value-at-stake issues and opportunities facing the company, the strategic and organizational alternatives available to each major business, and what will be required to implement these changes. In doing so, these chief executives have enabled their directors to be much more effective representatives of the company's shareholders.

BUILDING AN OWNERSHIP CULTURE

Putting in place the core beliefs and organizational conditions that we have discussed in this chapter goes a long way to establishing a culture where:

- Manager and shareholder interests are aligned.
- There is complete agreement throughout the company on the definition of winning and measure of success.
- Decisions are based on a factual understanding of customer needs and business economics.
- There is a drive to be profitably differentiated from the competition.
- There is zero tolerance for value-consuming investments.
- Growth is seen as a consequence of profitability, not a cause.
- There is a bias for action and an aggressive drive to maximize shareholder value, not just create it.

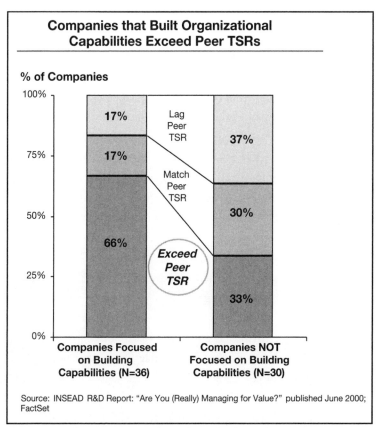

Figure 6.14: Companies that Built Organizational Capabilities Exceed Peer TSRs

However, to state the obvious, cultural change is difficult.

"People like the status quo," says Sir Brian Pitman of Lloyds. "They like the way it was. When you start changing things, the good old days look better and better. You've got to be prepared for massive resistance." Overcoming that resistance requires constant communication and reinforcement.

"When I was at Coca-Cola, I learned that old adage: everything communicates," says Don Knauss. "If I stay on message—and, oh by the way, we pay according to that message—guess what? The message gets constantly reinforced.

"You need to work on both strategic and organizational change simultaneously, and spend considerable time making sure everyone understands the overriding objective behind the pending changes."

Travis Engen concurs. "Everyone must know what is being changed and why. You need to make a big investment on the front end. While it is quicker to change out a bunch of people, you can't change out the entire organization. So you make the investment on the front end to communicate the objectives, and the whys behind the objectives, and you need to do it in a way that makes sense to everyone, so they will get behind it. Yes, it takes a little more time. But the payoff is worth it."

If you don't make the initial effort, you will find the buy-in and the follow-through lacking organization-wide, and the implementation will never go as smoothly or effectively as you want.

Miles White, Chairman and CEO of Abbott Labs, agrees. He also notes, "To make changes of this magnitude, you need to recognize this is about changing the way you manage the company. It's decision processes. It's what you measure. It's what you reject. It's what you reward. You have to be consistent with everything."

White reminds us, "All organizations have their habitual DNA, so migrating away from those past practices and toward the new ones you want takes time. It takes more time than you would like. And while you're going through the transition, people within the organization have the tendency to hang onto older practices because they're safe and understood. That slows you down and it's a competitive, tough world. You don't want that.

"How do you get your management teams to move faster? You keep putting in front of them the same themes, the same tests, the same metrics, the same measures, the same comparisons. You prod them with the benchmarks of either competitors or what's possible. And you push. You push with incentives and with what you talk about, and what you emphasize in your staff meetings. It's one hundred different things. But it's got to be consistent. You've got to keep a certain urgency around it."

• •

SUMMARY AND KEY TAKEAWAYS

• •

▸ Performance over time is the result of the beliefs and organizational conditions that have been established in a company.

▸ There are six interdependent organizational characteristics that influence behavior and performance:
   –Governing objective of the company
   –Roles and responsibilities
   –Business boundaries
   –Decision standards and processes
   –Incentives and rewards
   –Education and capabilities development

▸ Given the importance of these organizational conditions, top management needs to ensure they are designed and implemented in a way that aligns employee behavior with shareholder interests.

▸ With these conditions in place, managers across the company consistently make better decisions more efficiently and effectively than their competition, and, as a result, these companies are able to outperform their peers in customer and capital markets over extended periods of time.

CHAPTER 7
Pulling It All Together: Change-Management Blueprints and Timelines

- Implementing this level of strategic and organizational change requires a centrally designed and orchestrated change-management blueprint.

- Corporate-wide implementation should take no more than twelve to twenty-four months, even in the largest and most complex corporations.

- Maintaining the discipline needed to sustain superior shareholder value growth is a continuous undertaking.

- The results achieved are significant and enduring, creating a legacy that is worth all the effort.

The level of strategic and organizational change that is often required for companies to achieve and sustain superior shareholder returns cannot be well managed without a centrally designed and orchestrated change-management blueprint, coupled with a sense of urgency.

That urgency is key. Even though we are talking about significant change, it must be accomplished quickly. The best companies are successful in implementing these changes within twelve to twenty-four months. Any longer and the window of opportunity will close. Institutional resistance to change will overcome any effort that does not overwhelmingly demonstrate its merits within two years.

Let's quickly review the major components of the change-management program, and then provide an example of how they were implemented in one of the world's most successful corporations.

CHANGE-MANAGEMENT BLUEPRINT

The change-management blueprint is the "Master Plan" for directing, coordinating, and tracking the transformation process. It lays out:

- What strategic and organizational decisions and actions must be taken.
- The sequence and pace of those actions, and major milestones that must be reached.
- How and when to communicate to both internal and external constituents.

The plan is owned by the CEO and the executive committee, and it is their responsibility to see that it is executed. Figure 7.1 highlights the key components of the strategic and organizational change process as well as the communication and education steps that should accompany that process.

KEY SUCCESS FACTORS AND COMMON PITFALLS

Having helped over thirty large, complex companies design and manage the strategic and organizational changes needed to achieve

		"Creating the Conditions" (6 months)	"Taking the Actions" (12 to 18 months)
Organizational Conditions	**Clarify Definition of Winning and Measure of Success**	• Establish economic profit growth goals in line with top quartile superior shareholder returns	• Establish annual target-setting process
	Establish Clear, Consistent Governance Conditions – boundaries & structure – roles & responsibilities – incentives & rewards	• Define business units & segments for which financial and strategic information will be required • Clarify role of BU and Corporate Center • Remove impediments and increase incentives to grow economic profit	• Implement BU boundary and management structure changes where needed • Implement economic profit-based management incentives
	Improve Decision Standards and Processes – strategic – resource allocation – performance management	• Define minimum financial and strategic information standards • Define strategic decision process and decision criteria • Establish segment level operating and financial performance reporting	• Routinize collection, processing, and reporting of information essential to decision making • Adopt a rolling quarterly strategic performance management process
Strategic & Resource Allocation Change	**Develop Financial and Strategic Fact Base and Define Highest Value-at-Stake Issues & Opportunities**	• Develop corporate-wide fact base on the sources and drivers of corporate shareholder value • Commit to agenda of highest value-at-stake issues for resolution	• Begin updating value-improvement agenda • Evaluate closely related market and segment for possible expansion and related companies that are not being managed for shareholder value for potential acquisition
	Develop and Allocate Resources to Value Maximizing Business Strategies	• Demonstrate impact in a few "pilot" business units to build understanding and commitment and establish line champions	• Use "pilot" BUs to establish repeatable strategic decision template and roll-out across all BUs • Implement BU strategies • Begin redeploying capital from value-consuming to value-creating businesses and segments
Communication & Capabilities Development	**Internal and External Communication Plan**	• Internal (management, board) communication of: – governing objective – performance metrics, standards and targets – decision principles – highest value-at-stake issues & opportunities	• External (analyst, investor) communication of: – governing objective – performance metrics, standards, and targets – strategy & resource allocation decisions and actions
	Training and Capabilities Development	• Begin internal management education sessions • Utilize personnel staffed on "pilot" BU efforts to train other BU managers	• Establish corporate strategic management officer and build trained staff in all BUs • Link value management capabilities to career progression

Figure 7.1: Typical Components of a Change-Management Blueprint

and sustain superior shareholder performance, we have witnessed firsthand both the keys to success and common pitfalls companies experience in implementing these changes.

The sequencing and pace of corporate transformation programs will vary depending upon the circumstances of each individual company, specifically the:

- Complexity of the portfolio and strategic issues.
- Degree of organizational change required.
- Existing corporate culture.

That said, there are several characteristics common to all successful corporate transformations, namely:

- Ownership and involvement of top management.
- Early involvement and commitments of key line managers.
- Simultaneous and balanced progress in:

    –Making the strategic and resource-allocation decisions that produce tangible "bottom-line" performance improvement.

    –Establishing the organizational conditions needed to effectively manage shareholder value.

- Early results that provide evidence of the benefits and a template for others to follow.
- Formal communication plan and educational program.
- Performance mindset and bias toward action.

There are also common implementation pitfalls that must be avoided if you are to be successful. The CEOs featured in this book have emphasized that top management must not:

- Compromise on the definition of winning by adopting *a priori* strategic objectives that are not aligned with maximizing shareholder value.

- Believe that changes in measurement and incentives, alone, will produce the desired results.

- Believe that gradual change reduces risks; you have a limited window of opportunity to change your organization before the institution's resistance to change overwhelms your efforts.

- Focus on too many issues—shareholder value is concentrated, as are the opportunities to materially improve shareholder value.

- Underestimate the level of organizational change that will be needed for your organization to sustain superior shareholder performance.

Implementing the Blueprint at One of the World's Most Successful Corporations

Coca-Cola is acknowledged across the world as one of the most successful corporations. Its brands are recognized by every culture, and its products are within arm's reach of much of the world's population. For the majority of the last thirty years, it has also been one of the best managed companies in the world, delivering exceptional returns for its shareholders. Coca-Cola's exceptional performance is rooted in a set of beliefs that were instilled in the organization by one the world's most accomplished and successful chief executives, Roberto Goizueta. And when Coca-Cola has stumbled, it has been when management deviated from those beliefs and behaviors. It is both useful and inspirational to read Goizueta's statement of these beliefs in the company's 1997 annual report, which is transcribed below.

Why Shareowner Value?[8]

"At The Coca-Cola Company, our publicly stated mission is to create value over time for the owners of our business. In fact, in our society, that is the mission of any business: to create value for its owners.

Why? The answer can be summed up in three reasons.

First, increasing shareowner value over time is the job our economic system demands of us. We live in a democratic capitalist society, and here, people create specific institutions to help meet specific needs. Governments are created to help meet civic needs. Philanthropies are created to help meet social needs. And companies are created to help meet economic needs. Business distributes the lifeblood that flows through our economic system not only in the form of goods and services, but also in the form of taxes, salaries, and philanthropy.

Creating value is a core principle on which our economic system is based; it is the job we owe to those who have entrusted us with their assets. We work for our shareowners. That is—literally—what they have put us in business to do.

Saying that we work for our shareowners may sound simplistic—but we frequently see companies that have forgotten the reason they exist. They may even try in vain to be all things to all people and serve many masters in many different ways. In any event, they miss their primary calling, which is to stick to the business of creating value for their owners.

Furthermore, we must always be mindful of the fact that while a healthy company can have a positive and seemingly infinite impact on others, a sick company is a drag on the social order of things. It cannot sustain jobs, much less widen the opportunities available to its employees. It cannot serve customers. It cannot give to philanthropic causes.

And it cannot contribute anything to society, which is the second reason we work to create value for our shareowners: if we do our jobs, we can contribute to society in very meaningful ways. Our Company has invested millions of dollars in Eastern Europe since the fall of the Berlin Wall, and people there will not soon forget that we came early to meet their desires and needs for jobs and management skills. In the process, they are becoming loyal consumers of our products, while we are building value for our shareowners—which was our job all along.

Certainly, we—as a Company—take it upon ourselves to do good deeds that directly raise the quality of life in the communities in which we do business. But the real and lasting benefits we create don't come because we do good deeds, but because we do good work—work focused on our mission of creating value over time for the people who own the Company. Among those owners, for example, are university endowments, philanthropic foundations, and other similar nonprofit organizations. If The Coca-Cola Company is worth more, those endowments are similarly enriched to further strengthen the educational institutions' operations; if The Coca-Cola Company is worth more, those foundations have more to give, and so on. There is a beneficial ripple effect throughout society.

Please note that I said creating value 'over time,' not overnight. Those two words are at the heart of the third reason behind our mission: focusing on creating value over the long term keeps us from acting shortsighted.

I believe shareowners want to put their money in

companies they can count on, day in and day out. If our mission were merely to create value overnight, we could suddenly make hundreds of decisions that would deliver a staggering short-term windfall. But that type of behavior has nothing to do with sustaining value creation over time. To be of unique value to our owners over the long haul, we must also be of unique value to our consumers, our customers, our bottling partners, our fellow employees, and all other stakeholders—over the long haul.

Accordingly, that is how the long-term interests of the stakeholders are served—as the long-term interests of the shareowners are served. Likewise, unless the long-term interests of the shareowners are served, the long-term interests of the stakeholders will not be served. The real possibility for conflict, then, is not between shareowners and stakeholders, but between the long-term and the short-term interests of both. Ultimately, everyone benefits when a company takes a long-term view. Ultimately, no one benefits when a company takes a short-term view.

The creation of unique value for all stakeholders, including shareowners, over the long haul, presupposes a stable, healthy society. Only in such an environment can a company's profitable growth be sustained. Thus, the exercise of what is commonly referred to as 'corporate responsibility' is a supremely rational, logical corollary of a company's essential responsibility to the long-term interests of its shareowners. A company will only exercise this essential responsibility effectively if it promotes that social well-being necessary for a healthy business environment. It is as irrational to suppose that a company is primarily a welfare agency as it is to suppose that a company should not be concerned at all about the social welfare. Both views sacrifice the long-term common good to short-term benefits—whether shareowner benefits or stakeholder benefits.

Certainly, harsh competitive situations can sometimes call for harsh medicine. But in the main, our shareowners look to us to deliver sustained, long-term value. We do that by building our businesses and growing them profitably.

At The Coca-Cola Company, we have built our business and grown it profitably for more than 110 years, because we have remained disciplined to our mission.

Not long ago, we came up with an interesting set of facts: a billion hours ago, human life appeared on Earth. a billion minutes ago, Christianity emerged. A billion seconds ago, the Beatles changed music forever. A billion Coca-Colas ago was yesterday morning.

The question we ask ourselves now is: what must we do to make a billion Coca-Colas ago by this morning? By asking that question, we discipline ourselves to the long-term view.

Ultimately, the mission of this Atlanta soft-drink salesman—and my 26,000 associates—is not simply to sell an extra case of Coca-Cola. Our mission is to create value over the long haul for the owners of our Company.

That's what our economic system demands of us. That's what allows us to contribute meaningfully to society. That's what keeps us from acting shortsighted. As businessmen and businesswomen, we should never forget that the best way for us to serve all our stakeholders—not just our shareowners, but our fellow employees, our business partners, and our communities—is by creating value over time for those who have hired us.

That, ultimately, is our job."

When it comes to managing shareholder value growth, there are very few CEOs as accomplished as Roberto Goizueta. In 1981, Goizueta, then head of Coca-Cola's supply chain, was chosen as the successor to then CEO, J. Paul Austin.

The choice was unusual. But so were the results. If you had invested $100 in Coca-Cola stock in 1981, when Goizueta first became CEO, it would have been worth $3,500 seventeen years later. (See Figure 7.2.)

Goizueta changed the culture of Coca-Cola by systematically changing the beliefs and the behaviors of the Coca-Cola employees, and therefore the results of the corporation. He did so by:

1. Redefining Winning and the Measure of Success

Goizueta was very clear about Coca-Cola's definition of winning. "Management's primary [governing] objective is to create as much value as possible for the company's shareholders," he said. "Management doesn't get paid to make the shareholders comfortable, we get paid to make them rich." And the way to make them rich, he said time after time, was by producing the most economic profit growth possible. Eventually, every employee of the Coca-Cola Company understood the importance of growing economic profits and increasing shareholder value.

At Coca-Cola, Goizueta moved quickly to drive strategic and organizational changes needed to reinvigorate economic profit growth.

2. Leveraging the Fact That Shareholder Value Was Concentrated

Goizueta recognized that Coca-Cola's previous efforts to grow earnings through diversification—buying a movie studio, expanding into the wine business, and even operating a shrimp farm—had been an unmitigated disaster for its shareholders. As a result, he got rid of those businesses and focused the corporation on the beverage business where Coca-Cola had a competitive advantage and could

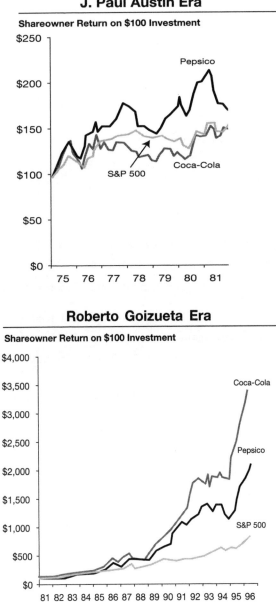

J. Paul Austin Era

Shareowner Return on $100 Investment

Roberto Goizueta Era

Shareowner Return on $100 Investment

Figure 7.2: Coca-Cola Shareholders Returns, Before and During the Goizueta Years

Source: FactSet

generate economic profit growth. Moving from the "old" corporate strategy of diversification to his new model of profitable growth through focus and differentiation required a very clear agenda to keep the organization on track.

3. Establishing and Managing an Explicit Value-Improvement Agenda

Over the next several years, Coca-Cola management followed a straightforward value-improvement agenda. It included:

- Eliminating unprofitable growth.
- Developing differentiated strategies to maximize profitable growth.
- Differentially investing resources in infrastructure development.

Goizueta's approach here was thorough and relentless. Every division was evaluated against an ultimate standard: "is it contributing to shareholder-value growth, and if it is not, what must be done so that it does?"

And if no answer can be found, the division was divested, as Figure 7.3 makes clear.

4. Developing and Deploying Differentiated Strategies and Differential Allocation of Resources

Coca-Cola relentlessly pursued those strategies that maximized economic profit growth, including:

- Brand proliferation
- Geographic expansion
- Market development
- Capturing profitable market share

Year	Divestiture	Rationale	Comments
1981	• Aqua-Chem industrial boilers and water treatment	• Industrial customers poor fit with Coca-Cola's consumer products focus	• Division where Goizueta initially worked and eventually managed
1982	• Instant coffee & tea division	• Subpar returns of 7–8%	• Sold for book value
1983	• Wine divisions	• Eroding market economics	• Sold for slightly more than book value
1984	• Ronco Pasta Makers	• Subpar returns of 7–8%	
1985	• Flexible Products plastic containers	• Subpar returns of 7–8%	
1986	• Columbia Pictures	• Subpar returns	• Original acquisition driven by Goizueta
1989	• Belmont Springs bottled water	• Subpar returns	• $61M gain before income tax

Source: FactSet

Figure 7.3: Coca-Cola's Divestiture Strategy, 1981–1989

Figure 7.4 shows at a glance what Goizueta and his management team did when it came to profitably expanding the company's brands.

The way Goizueta expanded geographically was just as well thought out. Coca-Cola pursued a systematic expansion model for entering, developing, and gaining a leading position in new geographic markets, as illustrated in Figure 7.5.

The managers of every single market where Coca-Cola competed were charged with increasing per capital consumption of Coca-Cola products and economically profitable sales. Figure 7.6 presents a five-year snapshot of just how well they responded.

As you can see, the company's growth rate was faster than the competition's in most cases. But, again, increasing profitable growth, not just top-line growth, was the goal. (See Figure 7.7.)

Fundamental to Coca-Cola's geographic expansion and market development was its approach to establishing, expanding, and managing its global bottler network. By 1995, Coca-Cola's infrastructure investments had resulted in enormous growth in highly profitable concentrated volume while creating more than $1.2 billion in direct capital gains. (See Figure 7.8.)

How did Goizueta accomplish this at Coca-Cola? Most importantly, he changed the Coca-Cola culture and its organizational capabilities to make sure that the company was not only focused on increasing shareholder value but that it had the requisite financial, strategic, and organizational skills, knowledge, and training to achieve that goal. (See Figure 7.8.)

Finally, Goizueta and his senior management team provided constant reinforcement along the way to prevent the organization from drifting back into its old ways—both directly and though more subtle but effective means, like the many video screens placed around the corporate offices flashing updates of Coca-Cola's stock price.

Did all this effort pay off?

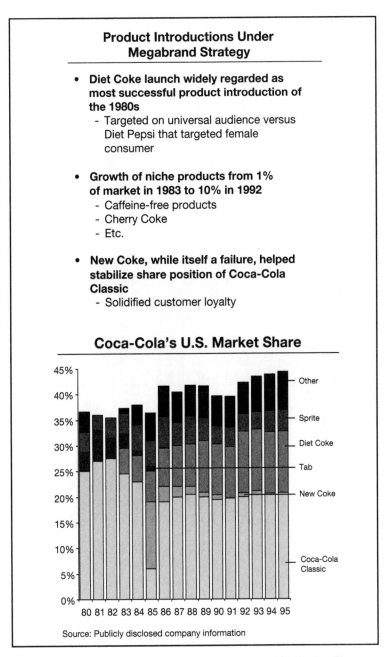

Product Introductions Under Megabrand Strategy

- **Diet Coke launch widely regarded as most successful product introduction of the 1980s**
  - Targeted on universal audience versus Diet Pepsi that targeted female consumer

- **Growth of niche products from 1% of market in 1983 to 10% in 1992**
  - Caffeine-free products
  - Cherry Coke
  - Etc.

- **New Coke, while itself a failure, helped stabilize share position of Coca-Cola Classic**
  - Solidified customer loyalty

Coca-Cola's U.S. Market Share

Source: Publicly disclosed company information

Figure 7.4: Coca-Cola Product Introductions and U.S. Market Share, 1981–1995

	New Markets	Emerging Markets	Leading Edge Markets
Consumer Marketing	• Establish single-brand awareness (predominately through signage)	• Broaden communication channels	• Saturate media • Saturate point of purchase
Customer Marketing	• Primarily retail outlet availability • Competitively price	• Expand availability beyond major population centers • Introduce point-of-sale promotion	• Achieve ubiquity – Multiple location in-store merchandising – Expand vending
Product Packaging	• Single-serve offering to promote trial	• Expand SKU portfolio • Encourage consumption through larger package sizes and per-ounce value	• Expand home consumption through multi-packs • Encourage impulse purchase through specialized packaging
Packaging Distribution & Sales Infrastructure	• Form alliance, JV or acquire well-capitalized bottler with capabilities and visibility • Establish high-population-center coverage	• Adjust bottler structure and ownership to allow maximum infrastructure growth • Achieve market-wide distribution coverage	• Rationalize production/distribution system and ownership structure to achieve low cost/investment • Establish anchor bottler • Build supply capabilities for new markets

Figure 7.5: Coca-Cola's Model for Entering New Markets

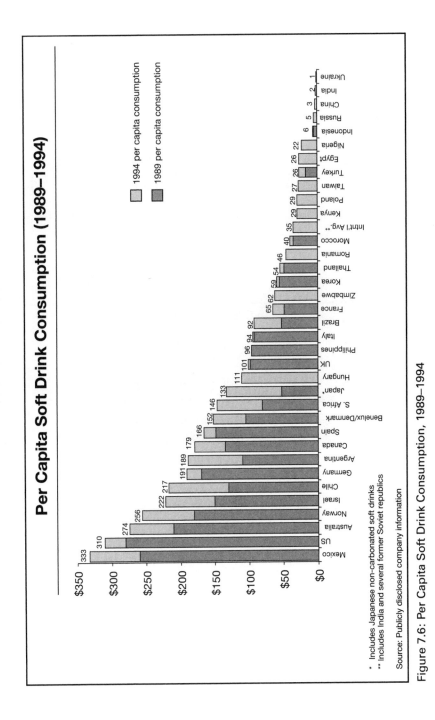

Figure 7.6: Per Capita Soft Drink Consumption, 1989–1994

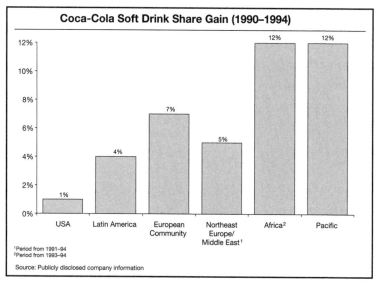

Figure 7.7: Coca-Cola Soft Drink Share Gain, 1990–1994

The Payoff

As a result of the strategic, organizational, and cultural transformation that Goizueta led, Coca-Cola's revenue, operating profits, economic profits, and total shareholder returns (stock price appreciation plus dividend yield) expanded dramatically. Total return to shareholders during his seventeen-year tenure was an astounding annual rate of 27 percent. (See Figure 7.10.)

Such performance is the ultimate evidence of the capabilities of this chief executive. And the results that can be achieved when the right beliefs and behaviors are established across a corporation.

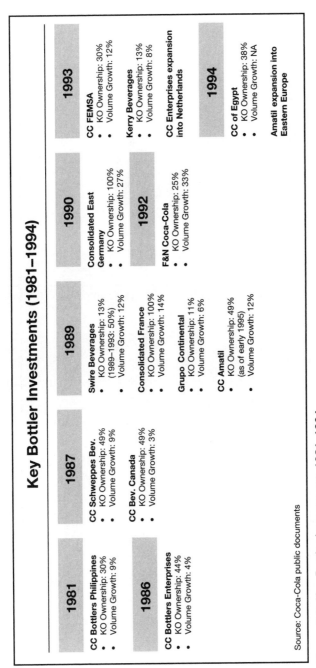

Key Bottler Investments (1981–1994)

1981

CC Bottlers Philippines
- KO Ownership: 30%
- Volume Growth: 9%

1986

CC Bottlers Enterprises
- KO Ownership: 44%
- Volume Growth: 4%

1987

CC Schweppes Bev.
- KO Ownership: 49%
- Volume Growth: 9%

CC Bev. Canada
- KO Ownership: 49%
- Volume Growth: 3%

1989

Swire Beverages
- KO Ownership: 13% (1989–1993: 50%)
- Volume Growth: 12%

Consolidated France
- KO Ownership: 100%
- Volume Growth: 14%

Grupo Continental
- KO Ownership: 11%
- Volume Growth: 6%

CC Amatil
- KO Ownership: 49% (as of early 1995)
- Volume Growth: 12%

1990

Consolidated East Germany
- KO Ownership: 100%
- Volume Growth: 27%

1992

F&N Coca-Cola
- KO Ownership: 25%
- Volume Growth: 33%

1993

CC FEMSA
- KO Ownership: 30%
- Volume Growth: 12%

Kerry Beverages
- KO Ownership: 13%
- Volume Growth: 8%

CC Enterprises expansion into Netherlands

1994

CC of Egypt
- KO Ownership: 38%
- Volume Growth: NA

Amatil expansion into Eastern Europe

Source: Coca-Cola public documents

Figure 7.8: Key Bottler Investment, 1981–1994

Organizational Capabilities	Financial Capabilities	Strategic Capabilities
• Established shareowner value maximization as governing objective	• Began measuring economic profit and key value drivers for every business unit	• Top-down, multi-year volume and profitability targets
• Instituted incentive compensation plan based on economic profit and shareowner-return performance	• Established continuous twelve-month rolling estimate of financial performance	• Significant investment and utilization of market and competitor intelligence
• Centralized global marketing while decentralizing operations management and financial accountability	• Instituted financial management policies to maximize shareowner returns	• Established center-led and BU-implemented strategy development and review process linked to resource allocation
• Restructured bottler ownership position while maintaining control over activity chain		

Figure 7.9: Coca-Cola's Capabilities-Driven Approach to Value Management

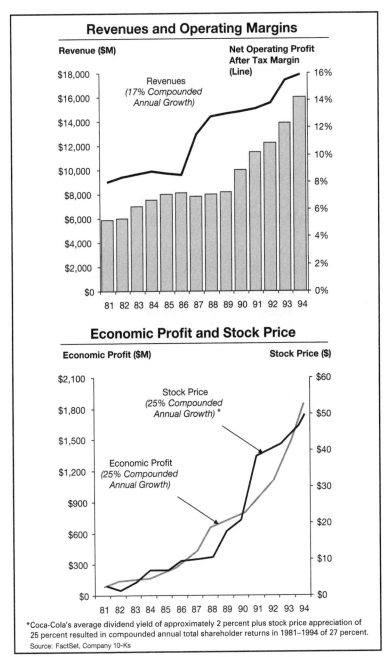

Figure 7.10: Coca-Cola's Financial and Shareholder Return Results, 1981–1994

. . . .
SUMMARY AND KEY TAKEAWAYS
. . . .

▸ The kind of leadership displayed by Roberto Goizueta and all other successful CEOs referenced in this book is essential for any company hoping to outperform its peers on an ongoing basis.

▸ Changing the way large and complex companies are managed starts by changing beliefs and by concurrently upgrading the organizational conditions that influence behaviors.

▸ Managing this level of change in large, complex companies requires a centrally designed and orchestrated change-management blueprint—a clear and consistent plan that guides the change-management process over a twelve- to twenty-four-month period.

▸ The customer and capital market results that are achieved and sustained as a consequence of institutionalizing the right beliefs and behaviors are one of the great legacies of successful CEOs.

Closing Comments

And there you have it.

You knew going in that beliefs drive behaviors and behaviors drive results. What you may have not appreciated are the various management misperceptions that can limit a company's performance. Overcoming these misconceptions and establishing the right beliefs and organizational conditions are at the heart of achieving a competitive advantage in both the customer and capital markets and sustaining superior shareholder value growth. There are five core beliefs that are held by those executives that have sustained superior shareholder returns over time. These executives:

1. Believe that winning is ultimately defined by the returns a company delivers to its shareholders.

All good leaders understand that no group of individuals can be aligned unless there is a common definition of *winning* and an agreed-upon *measure of success*. Leaders at shareholder-value-managed companies define *winning* as outperforming their peers in total shareholder return over time.

These leaders recognize that in order to deliver superior shareholder returns, their company must do a better job than its competition at both (1) creating customer value and (2) capturing the optimal portion of that value for the company's shareholders. These leaders recognize that earnings growth alone is not sufficient to create shareholder value. While there are several important internal measures of performance, there is only one performance measure that defines success in both the customer and capital markets—the company's share of the economic profits.

That is why successful businesses generate more economic profit growth over time than their competitors. Successful leaders recognize that improved measurements alone will not deliver improved results. They know that in order to deliver superior shareholder value, managers must have both the incentive and the know-how to outperform investor expectations.

2. Believe that shareholder value is always highly concentrated.

Hard as it may be to believe at first, in many corporations, less than 40 percent of employed capital generates more than 100 percent of the company's stock price, while 25 percent to 35 percent of employed capital is actually destroying shareholder value! Shareholder value *is always* highly concentrated. This concentration offers tremendous leverage to those managers who are willing to unlock the latent shareholder value potential that exists in all corporations.

Not all market share points are equally valuable. Managers need to understand the economic profit contribution of each point of market share in order to make good strategic and resource allocation decisions. When managers develop this understanding they can better focus their strategies and resources on growing economically profitable segments of their business while fixing, or withdrawing, resources from economically unprofitable ones.

Focus and differentiation will enable your company to gain and maintain a leading share of economic profits in the markets it chooses to serve. By doing so, the company will establish a reinvestment advantage that is difficult, if not impossible, for competitors to match. And it is competitive advantage, not diversification, that reduces risk and maximizes shareholder value.

3. Believe you must actively manage to a value-improvement agenda.

Companies have only a limited number of opportunities to make a material impact on shareholder value. Knowing what those five to ten opportunities are, and focusing management time and attention on them, is what turns good companies into great ones. By clearly defining the highest value-at-stake issues and opportunities facing the company, managers are able to focus time and resources on those things that will materially change performance. It is the primary means by which true value-oriented CEOs guide their company. In doing so, they are acting just as an activist investor would.

It takes extreme discipline to remain focused on the top strategic issues and not allow what is urgent or popular to replace issues that are critical for maximizing shareholder value over time.

4. Believe that only differentiated strategies and differential allocation of resources lead to superior performance.

Good companies do things better; superior companies do things differently.

Material gains in both economic profit growth and shareholder value come from fundamental improvements in the choices about *where* and *how* to compete, and redirecting resources to those opportunities with the highest potential for growing shareholder value. Your managers need to recognize that strategic innovations—changes in their business models—can be as valuable as product innovations in producing superior performance in both the customer and capital markets.

5. Believe that organizational advantage is the ultimate source of sustainable competitive advantage.

The goal of delivering and sustaining superior shareholder value growth is ultimately about building an ownership culture within your company, a culture where every employee thinks and acts as an entrepreneurial owner.

Corporate behaviors are influenced by the beliefs and organizational conditions (i.e., the governing objective, roles and responsibilities, business boundaries, decision standards, incentives, and capabilities) that exist within a company. If you want everyone to act like an owner, every aspect of the company must be sending that message.

Based on our years of experience in helping well managed companies achieve and sustain superior performance, we are certain the concepts covered in this book can help you and your management team significantly improve the shareholder value of your company. By establishing the right beliefs, your organization will overcome the misconceptions that are impeding performance, and you will establish the behaviors that will result in material improvements in customer and capital market performance.

Notes

1. All figures with the source note "FactSet" are created from data used with permission from FactSet Research Systems Inc.
2. Betsy Morris, "Roberto Goizueta and Jack Welch: The Wealth Builders: How A Patrician Cuban Emigre and a Train Conductor's Son Unlocked the Secrets of Creating Shareholder Value," *Fortune*, December 11, 1995.
3. Economic Profit = After-tax earnings minus a charge for the capital employed to generate those earnings. See Chapter 2 for a more thorough description of economic profit and its relationship to cash flow and shareholder value.
4. Warren Buffett, Berkshire Hathaway Inc., *Owner's Manual*, 1996.
5. Economic Value Added (EVA) is a trademark of Stern Stewart, LLC.
6. James M. Kilts, *Doing What Matters: How to Get Results That Make a Difference*, Crown Business, 2010.
7. Philippe Haspeslagh, Tomo Noda, and Fares Boulos, "Managing for Value: It's Not Just About the Numbers," Harvard Business Review, July–August, 2001, 64–73.
8. Coca-Cola Company, *Annual Report*, 1997.

About the Authors

Scott Gillis has spent over 25 years advising chief executives and board-level management on the strategic, resource allocation, and organizational changes needed to deliver superior shareholder returns. Scott cofounded Galt & Company, a top management advisory firm that has been associated with some of the more notable corporate success stories of the last two decades. Scott is a graduate of the Harvard Business School and holds a geophysical engineering degree from the Colorado School of Mines.

Lee Mergy is a cofounder of Galt & Company. For more than two decades, Lee has been helping senior management of Fortune 200 companies develop the strategies and organizational capabilities required to achieve and sustain superior shareholder returns. Lee has an MBA from the Yale School of Management and a BS in aerospace engineering from the University of Kansas.

Joe Shalleck is also a cofounder of Galt & Company. Over the last 20 years, Joe has helped companies develop and implement the capabilities required to effectively manage shareholder value. Joe earned an MBA from the Wharton School of Business and holds an industrial engineering degree from Lehigh University.